Praise for 50 W

"Helvarg's book does a great job connecting readers with the ocean and the many problems it faces. The author urges people to continue using the ocean for boating, fishing, surfing, etc., but offers clear, simple steps we can take to enjoy it in a more sustainable manner. Well-structured, with entertaining animation and a useful annotated list of references, *50 Ways* is a must-read for anyone and everyone who takes pleasure in the ocean environment."

—*Surf Life for Women*

"Combining wisdom and humor, scientific accuracy and artistic genius, Helvarg and Toomey show why the ocean matters to all of us, with clear answers to the crucial question, 'What can I do to help?' Everyone, from toddler to tycoon, can find inspiration for action in this must-have guide to ocean care."

—Sylvia Earle, Marine scientist, author and National Geographic Explorer-in-Residence

"My favorite chronicler of the environmental movement, David Helvarg has drafted a workable blueprint for grassroots action to save the seas."

—Robert Kennedy, Jr. President, Waterkeeper Alliance

"*50 Ways* is an invaluable tool for anyone who cares about preserving our precious marine environment. This simple book answers the tough question, 'How can I help save the oceans?'"

—Peter Benchley, Author of *Jaws*, and marine conservation advocate

"This is a great book—it makes saving the oceans fun and do-able (which it is, by the way)—can't wait to try out number 43 on my cousins."

—Ted Danson, Actor, Board member, Oceana

"Our oceans are in crisis. These great natural treasures can be saved if the nation is committed to their protection and each of us are committed to their preservation. This book is an important guide for the public to saving our oceans."

—Leon Panetta, Chair Pew Oceans Commission,
former White House Chief of Staff

"The ocean nurtures each and every one of us, without it human life cannot be sustained. So please read *50 Ways* and make it a part of your everyday life."

—Dr. Robert D. Ballard, author and discoverer of Titanic

50 ways to save the ocean

50

ways to
save the
ocean

David Helvarg

INNER OCEAN PUBLISHING
Maui • San Francisco

Inner Ocean Publishing, Inc.
P.O. Box 1239
Makawao, Maui, HI 96768-1239
www.innerocean.com

Illustrations by Jim Toomey
Cover design by Laura Beers
Book design by Madonna Gauding

Inner Ocean Publishing is a member of Green Press Initiative, a nonprofit program dedicated to supporting publishers in their efforts to reduce their use of fiber sourced from
endangered forests. We elected to print this title on 50% postconsumer recycled paper
with the recycled portion processed chlorine free.

As a result, we have saved the following resources:

27 trees, 1266 lbs of solid waste, 9855 gallons of water, 2374 lbs of net greenhouse gases,
19 million BTU's.

For more information on the Green Press Initiative, visit
http://www.greenpressinitiative.org.

PUBLISHER CATALOGING-IN-PUBLICATION DATA

Helvarg, David, 1951-
50 ways to save the ocean / David Helvarg ; illustrated by Jim
Toomey. — Maui, Hawai'i : Inner Ocean, 2006.
p. ; cm.
ISBN-13: 978-1-930722-66-8 (pbk.)
ISBN-10: 1-930722-66-4 (pbk.)
1. Marine resources conservation–United States.
2. Conservation of natural resources–United States. I. Toomey,
Jim P. II. Title. III. Fifty ways to save the ocean.
GC1020 .H45 2006
333.91/64160973–dc22 0604

Printed in the United States of America

05 06 07 08 09 10 DATA 10 9 8 7 6 5 4 3 2

DISTRIBUTED BY PUBLISHER'S GROUP WEST
For information on promotions, bulk purchases, premiums, or educational use, please
contact: 866.731.2216 or sales@innerocean.com.

Contents

Foreword

A Blue Earth Echo

If there's one thing I learned growing up in my family, it was that we as individuals need to protect the environment—not only by volunteering, donating money, or going on great adventures of discovery, as my grandfather and father have done, but also by making fundamental changes in our everyday habits. When considering your impact on the planet, realize that the critical concept is not that you can make a difference; it's that everything you do already does make a difference. That's a subtle but very important distinction. The first statement implies that by simply going about your everyday life you don't have any real impact on the environment; not until you make a particular effort do you finally "make a difference." The truth is, everything you do makes a difference, and all of your actions have consequences. Things as simple as what kind of toilet paper you buy or where you choose to get married (on the beach, for instance; see action 2) have a ripple effect—an echo that resounds from your life and then, in unforeseen ways, comes back to enrich it or degrade it.

We have all heard the saying "think globally, act locally," and it's true that our actions have far-reaching effects beyond our own local sphere of influence. When we choose to buy organic produce (see action 12) or to eat responsible seafood (action 13), we send a message to industry that organic, responsible, and humane food is important to customers and thus to its bottom line. Believe me, as Bono, the lead singer of U2, says, "Shopping is politics." When any of us makes a decision as a consumer, that decision is recorded, numbered, and noted in some office in some town in some place that we may never have heard of—but I guarantee that what we don't see does affect us.

We must each start by changing our own behavior, though that's not the end of our responsibility. To truly change the course of events, we must affect every person we come in contact with. For example, a good friend of mine recently eliminated all cleaning products that contain chlorine bleach and other harmful substances from her house. Now, every friend who visits gets a tour of her pantry and learns which environmentally friendly products have replaced the harmful ones.

That is her earth echo.

Now ask yourself: What is yours?

Of course, morals aren't the only reason to shop responsibly or act in a different way. Our health and the health of our children depend on it. More and more harmful substances, from polychlorinated biphenyls (PCBs) to mercury and lead, are found in our oceans and the creatures that inhabit them. Life on land and in the ocean is an intricate web that connects all creatures (action 39). As John Muir wrote, "When one tugs at a single thing in nature [one] finds it attached to the rest of the world."

Our oceans are in peril, and it is up to us to do something to save them. We cannot rely on some politician to fix the problem if we don't establish it as a fundamentally important issue. The primary job of politicians is to get reelected, not to be creative. They are, by nature, reactionary. We live in a country where ordinary citizens still have the power to influence the course of our nation. It is our responsibility to ensure that the environment is an issue of such importance that it can make or break a politician's career (action 49). National politics isn't the only political stage that matters either. Local politics, at the zoning board, for example (action 43), often has a critical impact on our lives.

The environment is not just about trees and birds and fish. It's about you and me, the future of our children, and the quality of our lives. For example, when the communities along the Hudson River first allowed General Electric to operate dangerous facilities because they would provide jobs in the area, those communities made a choice to benefit themselves over the short-term, and they have paid the price for that shortsighted perspective. After GE spent decades dumping PCBs into the river, hundreds of local fisherman were out of work, barge traffic became virtually nonexistent because shipping channels were too toxic to dredge, and thousands of people throughout the Hudson Valley accumulated dangerous levels of PCBs in their bodies. The health effects of PCBs include skin ailments, reproductive disorders, liver disease, and cancer. The worst part was that the choice people made (perhaps because they lacked the information they needed) had long-term negative effects not only on their own lives but also on those of their children, since these chemicals pass from pregnant women to fetuses.

As we expend more and more effort to extract fewer and fewer natural resources from our ocean planet, we miss the point that our duty is not to consume but to protect and conserve. We still mistakenly believe that the oceans are a never-ending resource, despite the fact that we have proved time and again that they are not. For those who argue that economic gain is the justification for ignoring environmental protection, evidence shows that the gain is illusory (the Hudson River Valley is only one example among many of how destroying the environment creates future economic downturn). Continuing to ignore our corrosive impact on this planet will have increasingly disastrous effects on our health, our economy, our security, and our society.

Despite our misguided actions in the past, today there is more reason to hope than ever. We stand at the dawn of an age in which we have access to information in ways that my father and grandfather never dreamed of, from cable television to the Internet to Web-enabled PDAs. The key is to realize that we are all responsible to act on that information in a positive and empowering way. I hope that we use our knowledge wisely and learn that we are tied to every living creature in one way or another, that none of us can live without a healthy planet. Each one of us has an earth echo; it defines our relationship with the planet and with each other.

Reading *50 Ways to Save the Ocean* is a great way to begin creating an earth echo that you can be proud of.

So, go on—head for the beach, and get started.

Philippe Cousteau
President, EarthEcho International

Introduction

....

"I really don't know why it is that all of us are so committed to the sea, except I think it's because in addition to the fact that the sea changes, and the light changes, and ships change, it's because we all come from the sea."

—President John F. Kennedy, 1962

"The reason why I love the sea I cannot explain. It's physical. When you dive, you begin to feel like you're an angel."

—Jacques Cousteau, 1997

The United States is and always has been an oceanic society. From the Bering Sea land bridge to the Jamestown Settlement to the processing lines at Ellis Island, we have been a tempest-tossed people, a saltwater people, a coastal people. We have lived well on the abundance of our seas and coastlines from the earliest canoe tribes setting fish traps along the Jersey shore to today's giant gantry crane operators unloading massive container ships at the Port of Long Beach/Los Angeles.

The United States owes much of its wealth, bounty, and heritage to the blue in our red, white, and blue. It provides us with oxygen to breath, is a driver of climate and weather, brings rain to our farmers, and food to our tables. It offers us recreation, transportation, protein, medicine, energy, security, and a sense of awe and wonder from sea to shining sea.

Evaporation from our oceans generates clouds and rain, which run down from our mountaintops in streams and rivers, following gravity through watersheds into bays, estuaries, salt marshes, mangrove swamps, sea grass meadows, kelp forests, coral reefs, seamounts (submerged mountains), submarine canyons, and, ultimately, the black deep plains of the abyss. From here, the waters begin their slow ascent back into our atmosphere, continuing the circulation that feeds the circle of life. This blue frontier is our final wilderness and sacred trust. We are, after all, the stewards of our blue-water planet.

Unfortunately, our seas are today in serious trouble, due to a host of problems linked to our behaviors. Marine wildlife has been overfished for the global seafood market. Careless coastal construction has destroyed salt marshes and other marine nurseries, filters, and storm barriers. Pollution from urban, industrial, and agricultural runoff is poisoning our seas, depleting them of oxygen, and making them more acidic. And climate change fired by our use of fossil fuels is bringing intensified storms, sea-level rises, beach erosion, and dying corals. Without wise coastal and energy planning we may face even more disasters like Hurricane Katrina.

"We used to say 'think globally and act locally.' But today the problems we face are local, regional, and global, so we have to respond at all levels at once," explains Steve Miller, as we strip off our dive gear. We're inside Aquarius, the world's only underwater science habitat. Aquarius is located next to a coral reef seven miles off Key Largo, Florida, and some 50 feet below the surface.

Steve is a director of the National Underseas Research Center, one of numerous marine science projects seeking to better understand the living design of our blue-marble planet. Unfortunately, the reef is dying around the yellow 48-foot-long cylindrical habitat that functions as both hostel and laboratory for visiting scientists. It's dying from coral diseases linked to polluted runoff from the land; physical contact from boats, anchors, and snorkelers; and bleaching from global warming. Still Steve remains optimistic that it's not too late to turn things around and restore the world's greatest wildlife range.

Aside from covering 71 percent of the earth's surface, the oceans contain more than 95 percent of the world's livable habitat. On land, animals make their homes between the underground burrows of prairie dogs and the treetop nests of birds. The oceans, by contrast, provide habitat for living from their surface waters, where turtles munch on jellyfish and sharks glide with their dorsal fins exposed, to the depths of the abyss, seven miles below, in the crushing, cold, black waters of the Marianas Trench in the Pacific. Here, fish, crabs, starfish, and other creatures earn their living from marine debris raining down from above or, amazingly, get their energy from hot sulfur vents spewing from the planet's core.

Until 1977, photosynthesis of sunlight was believed to be the basis for all life in the universe. That year scientists aboard a deep-diving research submarine off the Galapagos Islands discovered sulfurous hot-water vents 8,000 feet below the surface of the sea. The area around these vents was colonized by giant red-and-white tube worms, white crabs, clams, and other animals that contain sulfur-burning bacteria, which give them an alternative means of sustaining life. Today, NASA scientists believe similar "chemosynthetic" life-forms may exist around volcanic deep-water ocean vents beneath the icy crust of Jupiter's moon, Europa.

When I was a boy I used to look up at the stars and feel cheated that I was born a generation too soon to explore distant worlds such as Europa. But when I began to snorkel and scuba dive I realized that there are whole worlds of wonder right off our shores. The oceans are a largely uncharted and unexplored frontier wilderness, full of unseen mountain ranges, canyons, and deep abyssal plains. They are filled with unique species of "alien" life, many of which are only now being identified by scientists.

Many new oceanic discoveries, whether about the properties of soft corals in fighting cancer, the unexpected intelligence of octopuses, or the distribution of deep-water ocean vents, seamounts, and sponges, are unfolding at the same time that we are, unfortunately, destroying these resources. Ignorance and lack of interest about the ways we interact with our living oceans have led to abuses that threaten the saltwater crucible of our planetary experience.

While we like to think of ourselves as an explorer race, we also have to ask this ethical question: If we can't protect our own planet's living seas, what right do we have to seek out other worlds?

Problems such as offshore pollution, the impact of climate change on the sea, or the collapse of the world's fish, seabird, and turtle populations may seem too overwhelming for the average person. "What can I, my family, or my friends possibly do to effect change on such a scale?" you might wonder. Luckily, anthropologist Margaret Mead gave us the answer more than half a century ago: "Never doubt that a small group of dedicated people can change the world," she said. "Indeed, nothing else ever has."

This book suggests actions that each of us can take in the course of our daily lives to help assure the continued health of our coasts and oceans and to protect their wild and living waters. At the end of the book you will find contacts and resources for additional help in these activities. We can and should do this for our own sake, our children's sake, and the sake of all our fellow travelers on this miraculous ocean planet we call home.

David Helvarg
President, Blue Frontier Campaign

section

1

....

Enjoy

1. Go to the Beach

Enjoy the sand and the water and leave it as
clean or cleaner than you found it.

For many of us, our sense of wonder over our blue-marble
planet began with a trip to the beach. These days, despite
theme parks, shopping malls, and sports stadiums, going to the
beach remains the number one outdoor recreational activity for
all Americans, with some 68 million of us hitting the ocean
sand every year. The hot sand, the iodine-flavored sea air, the
thrill of cold waves on a hot day—or, conversely, warm, clear
waters on a muggy afternoon—are what "life is all about."
Boardwalks and umbrellas, French fries and hot dogs, gulls and
beach blankets, surf music syncopated by the thump of the
waves, body boards and skim boards, pelicans flying with their
wingtips to the waves, sandpipers skittering along the wet sand
at sunset—these familiar images and memories are to many of
us the very definition of leisure and renewal.

When children explore tide pools, pick up and examine
seashells along a golden shore, or build sand castles, they often
discover a spark of wonder that may inspire their life directions,
bringing them to science, architecture, engineering, or a range

of other callings. Looking out over a vast and seemingly unknowable ocean, or looking through a face mask into a world of brightly colored fish and corals, can also begin a child's transformation—the realization that each of us is part of something much larger than ourselves, something both mysterious and deeply attractive.

Mostly, though, beach time is about fun, family, friendship, and of course romance. The salty taste of the sea on our lips adds a tang of something sweet and special to long days whiled away without regret. Beach time is like living the good old days in the here and now.

To keep this time special we need to take care of the beaches we visit, whether for a day, a weekend, or a summer. Here are some commonsense precautions you can take to make sure the beach remains clean and natural for your future visits.

1. Take only pictures and leave only sand (carry out everything you carry onto the beach).

2. Wear waterproof sunscreen (you don't want to be a one-person oil spill, leaving sunscreen grease in the water).

3. Use the public restrooms, to keep the water clean.

4. Avoid swimming near storm-drain outlets, which can carry a mixture of pollutants into the water and increase your risk of getting sick by 57 percent, according to a major study.

5. Use walkovers to cross sand dunes, as opposed to walking through or jumping off the dunes themselves. Dunes help prevent beach erosion.

6. Keep your pet on a leash and away from areas frequented by marine wildlife, and make sure you clean up after your pet.

7. Don't chase or feed the wildlife.

8. Bring a trash bag with you, and pick up any litter you find.

2. Get Married on a Wild Beach

The places we associate with love are the
places we seek to conserve.

One morning my love and I were staying in a guest cabin above the ocean in Mendocino, California, when we were awakened by the sound of a bagpipe. We went out on our deck to see the two guests from the other cliff-top cabin with a preacher and a piper. They were standing out at the end of the bluff, getting married on the edge of the Pacific, with blue skies, white clouds, and blue and white waves acting as their witnesses.

I've been to a number of beach weddings, seaside family reunions, ceremonies to release the ashes of a relative into the ocean (human ashes are recyclable in the sea), and a memorial service for my life's love on her favorite beach. The ocean offers us both hope and solace, making us feel a part of something larger as we celebrate or commemorate the major turning points in our lives.

While all beaches have some level of wildness about them, wild beaches are those closest to a natural state, with ungroomed sands, driftwood, seaweed, or other wind- and wave-borne debris. They tend to be sparsely populated, have limited access, and draw colonies of seals or sea turtles as visitors. They can be found from Maine to Hawaii and are sometimes considered sacred by those who have lived longest by their side.

A certain wild passion and love of the sea draws people to make bonds of commitment by the ocean, from a first kiss in a sandstone cave (I still recall) to wedding vows on a windy beach. When our most memorable occasions take place at the beach, saving the sea becomes as personal as protecting the place where you found the love of your life. Here are a few suggestions about how to have an environmentally friendly wedding or special event at a beach:

1. Before planning, learn about beach regulations. Find out whether there's a maximum number of guests, whether food and drink are allowed, what noise and time restrictions exist, and whether you can pitch a tent.

2. Make sure you pack out anything you bring in and have secure hold-downs and storage bins so that nothing flies off into the water or tumbles down the beach. Littering is not romantic.

3. Know what the weather report and the tide tables say, and then be ready to enjoy any unexpected change.

4. Consider encouraging guests to offer wedding presents that give something back to the beach, such as contributions to your favorite shoreline protection group.

5. Vow to return to your wild beach to work to protect it, and cherish it as you do each other.

3. Dive Responsibly

Take only pictures and leave only bubbles,
while exploring underwater wonders.

It's been more than half a century since Jacques Cousteau and his friend Émile Gagnan invented the Self-Contained Underwater Breathing Apparatus (scuba) that allows a diver to swim freely and weightlessly through the water, and, in Cousteau's words, "feel like you're an angel." Today, diving and snorkeling have become hugely popular activities, with some 5 to 10 million Americans scuba-certified and 2 million actively diving on a regular basis. Among the certifying organizations that train people are the Professional Association of Diving Instructors (PADI) and the National Association of Underwater Instructors (NAUI). Both teach safe and responsible diving practices, and no one should don diving equipment without having passed these or similar professional courses.

Having become certified some 20 years ago, I've witnessed changing conditions on our reefs, in our kelp forests, and in many other parts of our ocean, usually not for the better. I've also found that, once exposed to the wonders of our seas—the colorful diversity and mind-boggling variety of life underwater—

divers and snorkelers often become leading advocates for the protection and restoration of marine wilderness.

Ironically, through careless behaviors, lack of experience, or lack of awareness, underwater visitors can also damage the very wonders they go below the surface to enjoy. In the early days, divers focused a lot on spearfishing and collecting. But sharp declines of abalone, sheepshead, and other once-popular marine prey in areas like California have taught local divers to be careful stewards of the marine wilderness they value. Today, far more divers are shooting pictures than spearguns as they seek ways to explore Jacques Cousteau's "silent world" without harming it. Here are some guidelines for protecting the seas while diving in them:

1. If you are diving or snorkeling from a boat, tie the boat to reef mooring buoys to prevent anchor damage to the living coral. If buoys have not been installed in the area, anchor in the sand a good distance from the reef, and make sure the anchor is secure, so that it doesn't drag.

2. Dive carefully so you don't harm corals and other organisms. A bump from a tank, knee, or camera can cause lasting damage. Keep your gauges and octopus (spare air source) secured, so they don't bump around.

3. Don't touch coral. A touch could remove a protective layer of "slime" and expose the polyps to diseases. (Also, many corals sting.)

4. Don't collect souvenirs. Dive sites can be rapidly depleted of their resources and beauty. Do collect discarded fishing line and other harmful human debris (see action 33), to protect the seascape you're enjoying.

5. If your dive site is crowded, ask your fellow divers or guide if they'd mind heading to a less crowded site. Crowds can negatively affect already stressed reefs.

6. When you join dive certification organizations, encourage them to include underwater environmental awareness and behavior in their training course curriculums.

7. Avoid the urge to hitch rides on turtles, manta rays, and other marine wildlife.

8. If you hunt or gather game such as lobsters, be sure to obey all fish and game laws.

4. Be a Blue Boater

Practice safe boating that protects both you and the ocean.

Sailing out to sea—far from land, or along its margins on bays, at reef lines, and in coastal waters—is a journey, a pleasure, and an adventure that humans have "embarked" on since they first devised barks that floated. A day on the water is a day almost certain to be remembered. I recall days of sunlight and mild winds with passing whales and dolphins riding our bow waves; and wilder days standing in harness on a flying outrigger till our catamaran pitch-poled, and I found myself underwater working my way through tangled lines and buckles. I remember slow paddles in hot mangrove backwaters; and pulling Gs on a roaring go-fast boat. I've enjoyed long sails on an outer reach and been shipwrecked on an empty desert strand. I don't regret a day, nor have I met many sailors who would trade their time on the water for any other endeavor.

There are now some 10 million recreational motorboats and millions more sailboats plying the ocean waters of the United States, everything from personal watercraft to classic wind-driven sloops to luxurious megayachts. In total the recreational boating industry generates some $30 billion a year in economic activity. It also generates far more pollution and other environmental and safety problems than most of its participants would like. Here are ways to assure that you and your friends act as smart, ocean-friendly sailors:

1. Make sure your boat has a fuel-efficient four-stroke engine or new direct-injection two-stroke engine that reduces exhaust emissions. Outmoded two-stroke personal watercraft and outboard engines are "stinkpots" fouling the air and releasing up to 2.5 million gallons of oil and gas into coastal waters every year.

2. Keep a supply of oil-absorbent rags on board for cleaning up small oil and fuel spills. Diapers also work well.

3. Anti-fouling agents can be foul. When painting or cleaning your boat, use legal bottom paints and biodegradable cleaning agents. Sand and scrape your boat at a distance from the water, and use a tarp or drop sheet to collect the old flakes for proper disposal.

4. Be aware that in most coastal areas it is illegal to use a power sander on bottom paint unless you tent your vessel.

5. Avoid discharging toilet waste. Use marina pump-out stations for your boat. Pet waste should be similarly disposed of, not tossed overboard.

6. Secure all items before heading out from the dock, and discard trash once you return to land. Plastic bags and Styrofoam pellets can be killers to birds, turtles, and other creatures that mistake them for food. If you lose trash overboard, especially if it's plastic, go back to retrieve it.

7. When cleaning fish, use a fish-cleaning station, or scatter the scales and offal at sea, not by the dock where they will attract scavengers. Alternatively, try composting the remains with peat moss or using them as a garden fertilizer.

8. Whenever possible, do business with ecofriendly marinas that have good management practices for containing and controlling pollution.

5. Keep Your Home Aquarium Ocean-Friendly

Make sure your saltwater tank reflects the ocean's wonders without depleting them.

"I gave up smoking and got addicted to aquariums," says Brian Harrison, owner of The Reef, a restaurant in Washington, DC, whose marine aquariums contain a mind-boggling assortment of neon-bright saltwater tropical fish. He's quick to explain that the fish, algae, and corals in his tanks are all captive-raised, grown by hand, either by himself or by other aquarists and dealers. None has been collected from coral reefs in the wild. Just as he wouldn't think of serving nonsustainable fish in his restaurant, he doesn't believe in keeping display fish unless they fit his ethic of marine protection.

Most people who keep saltwater or marine aquariums, including some 600,000 in the United States, do so because of their love for and fascination with these wondrous fish—and their reef or other ocean environments. But many don't realize that their hobby also affects coral reefs. More than 1,400 species of ornamental fish are traded worldwide, more than 20 million individual fish each year. Many tropical fish are captured though the use of cyanide, which is sprayed into coral caves and crevices to stun the fish. As a result half or more can die within hours of collection. Fish that are not targeted for sale are also killed, along with many coral polyps, and the coral's intricate marine ecosystem is damaged. With the high price tropical fish often command, too many are being removed from their home waters, including oceans off Hawaii and Florida. Fewer than 10 percent of marine ornamental species are currently captive-bred.

You can create an ecofriendly saltwater aquarium, but you have to do more than simply purchase whatever fish or rock coral catches your eye at your local pet store. Here are some guidelines for a sea-friendly aquarium:

1. Consider owning a freshwater aquarium. It is easy to set up and maintain one, and more than 90 percent of freshwater fish sold as pets are captive-raised. Some African cichlids rival the color and beauty of their marine cousins and breed readily in home aquariums.

2. If you own a marine aquarium, purchase tropical fish that have been reared in captivity. Aquacultured species you can now buy include clown fish, dottybacks, cardinal fish, gobies, batfish, sea horses, and several interesting invertebrates such as peppermint shrimp and snails. The group Reef Protection International produces a pocket guide to help you select sustainable aquarium fish (see Resources).

3. Join a hobby club or contact more experienced aquarists to learn how to captive-breed and trade your marine plants and animals. Several excellent online resources are available, such as Reef Central (www.reefcentral.com), where experts answer questions for new hobbyists.

4. Patronize aquarium shops that are environmentally aware. Hobby groups such as the Marine Aquarist Society (MAC) and advocacy groups such as Reef Protection International can help you locate them.

5. Ask about the origin of all fish you purchase. If they are not captive-bred by a company such as ORA, Inc., make sure they have MAC certification, which assures they were sustainably captured.

6. Never dump anything from your tank into a storm drain, lake, river, bay, or other body of water, because you could be introducing harmful non-native species or microbes (see action 25).

6. Go on a Whale-Watching Trip

The rescue of the great whales is a success story we can all learn from.

Some of my finest moments have been in the presence of whales: watching the great migration of gray whales along the Pacific Coast every year, watching humpbacks breaching off Hawaii and Alaska, watching the scimitar black dorsals of orcas on the hunt, the elongated bodies of seis, and the white doughy forms of belugas. Once, in Antarctica, the Zodiac raft I was in was bumped hard by a minke whale that then rolled out from under us. It was a real Melville moment. While other species of whales would "eye hop" (raise their heads out of the water) to stare curiously at us and our boats, the minkes were quick to flee at the sound of marine engines. Japanese whalers still hunt minkes in Antarctic waters, and the whales seem to know that the sound of engines can mean death from above.

During the 19th and well into the 20th century, the great whales of the world were hunted to near-extinction, first for their oil, which was the light source and lubricant of the machine age, and later for meat and other purposes. In 1982, following Save the Whales campaigns by Greenpeace and other conservation groups, the International Whaling Commission enacted a moratorium on commercial whaling. Both Norway and Japan have continued limited whaling (which they label "scientific"), and Iceland says it plans to resume whaling. Certain islanders, indigenous groups, and pirate whalers have also continued hunting small whales and dolphins.

Despite these threats, and other fatal encounters—with shipping traffic, fishing gear, military sonar, and other human disturbances—whale populations have been slowly rebounding since the ban on commercial whaling more than 20 years ago.

Today the great whales generate around a billion dollars a year worldwide for the whale-watching industry. Popular commercial whale-watching sites range from New England to California, Alaska to Hawaii, Spain to New Zealand. In the 21st century people have come to value whales as emblematic of ocean life and as fascinating sentient creatures, rather than simply as sources of oil and meat. That change in popular sentiment, understanding, and livelihood is also helping to change how we approach all the wondrous creatures that share our blue-marble planet. Here are some guidelines for safe whale-watching practices:

1. When boating in areas where whales and dolphins migrate or feed, minimize your speed in "no wake" zones, and avoid sudden turns.

2. Try to minimize the noise you generate around whales and dolphins.

3. Do not pursue, encircle, or come between whales, because these actions can stress the animals and may provoke aggressive (defensive) behavior on their part.

4. Approach animals from angles where they won't be taken by surprise, and adhere to local and federal rules on how close

you can come to whales. Keep at least 50 yards away, and allow your binoculars, spotting scope, or camera zoom lens to bring you "up close."

5. Don't overwhelm animals with large numbers of boats. If there are more than a few boats around a whale or pod of whales, back off (or encourage your captain to) and look elsewhere for other animals.

6. Choose a whale-watching boat operator who makes adequate safety provisions, has high standards of customer care, and employs an onboard naturalist, if possible. A growing number of nonprofit operators, such as the Pacific Whale Foundation and American Cetacean Society, combine whale watching with research and conservation.

7. Visit a Tide Pool

Learn what happens when the ocean and the shore
are mixed by the tides.

I was walking along the Point Loma tide pools in San Diego with my friend Charlie and his four-year-old son, Nick. Every few feet Nick would stop at the edge of a watery depression, point to a sea star, a small fish, a crab, or some waving fronds of seaweed and ask, "What's this, dude?"

The rocky intertidal zone where land and ocean meet is a window into the sea and a chance to discover some of its unique and complex life up close. During low tides, pools of trapped water form in rocky depressions. In these pools you can find flowery anemones, limpets, sea stars in many colors (orange, red, brown, pink, and purple), small blenny fish, spiky sea urchins, and sometimes an elusive octopus or other unusual creature.

Few animals in this dynamic, tidal-driven ecosystem can harm humans, but many are sensitive and can be harmed by us. The tide pools of California, for example, used to contain many large abalones clinging to the rocks along the surf zone, until they were stripped away for sale and consumption. Now, even though the taking of wild abalone is banned, it's rare to spot even a small one in these shallow waters. The same problem is occurring where people now collect mussels, sea palms, turban snails, and owl limpets for food from tide pools where this foraging is strictly prohibited.

The joy of discovery as you watch the behavior of predators and plant eaters, the chance to stroke a sea star, and the feel of a periwinkle snail crawling across your palm fascinate children and adults alike. The moment when water separates ropes of seaweed to reveal living dramas no more than a yard across and as transient as the turning of a tide can both educate and inspire. Here's how you can capture the wonder while assuring that it will remain to be discovered anew:

1. When visiting tide pools, step carefully to avoid slipping and falling. Wear shoes with good traction and clothes you don't mind getting wet.

2. Start your visit at least one hour before low tide, and keep an eye on the water, so you don't get trapped with the incoming tide.

3. Avoid stepping on animals or clumps of seaweed, which might be hiding crabs and other creatures.

4. After you've turned rocks over and examined what's under them, carefully turn them back to their original position so as not to dislodge small creatures.

5. Don't remove animals attached to rocks, such as sea anemones and barnacles, from the tide pool.

6. Return crabs, sea stars, snails, and other creatures to the pool location where you found them. Do not remove fish and other creatures that need to remain in the water to survive.

7. Ask a local ranger or naturalist about the life you're seeing.

8. Don't take home any "souvenirs."

9. If you see anyone stealing animals or edible seaweeds from a protected tide pool (where warning signs are posted) report them to a local ranger. If none is around, take down a license plate number, and file a report.

8. Take Kids Surfing, or Have Them Take You

Surfing and bodyboarding (or boogie boarding) are nonconsumptive ways to enjoy the ocean.

He'e nalu or "wave sliding" is how the old Hawaiians described the ancient Polynesian sport that later became known as surfing. For a time, the practice was *kapu* (taboo), meaning that only Hawaiian royalty could take to the waves, because of fear that peasants would abandon their work in the taro fields for the pure pleasure of catching waves.

Today's surfing is equally exhilarating. Instead of long planks of dense wood, surfboards are now made of fiberglass-covered foam cores with fins and leashes for maintaining control and connection.

Some people, like me, prefer to bodysurf unencumbered, while many enjoy the relative ease of bodyboarding. Some board surfers like to shred waves using short, highly maneuverable "sticks" while others go with the flow on soul-surfing long boards. The world's handful of big wave surfers who hang out in places with names like Jaws, Killers, and Mavericks use nine-to eleven-foot "guns" or "rhinos" to ride giants. More recent wave riders include sailboarders, kite-surfers, and seagoing kayakers, who hark back to the first Polynesian outrigger fishermen who realized that wave riding wasn't just a quick way to bring their catch home but also serious fun.

As wonderful as it is to catch waves, modern "wave sliders" are also affected by damage to the seas. Today "standing waves" formed by point breaks and other unique ocean formations are endangered by development of marinas, seawalls, and other human structures. Surfers who plunge into the water to get their stoke (intense pleasure) may come out with infections and diseases from water-borne pollution or clinging tar from oil pollution. One response has been to form groups such as the Surfrider Foundation, which is made up of tens of thousands of surfers and other water-loving people who fight the destruction of our seas.

Observers and participants from Captain Cook to Lord Byron to the Beach Boys have noted the wonders of surfing. It is a totally renewable use of the sea but one, like so many, that we have to work to protect. Here are a few ways you can both surf and protect the waves.

1. Pick up any litter you encounter on the beach or in the water.

2. Find out if it's safe to surf in your area (or the area you're visiting) after it rains. In areas such as southern California with high levels of polluted runoff, many surfers stay out of the water for 72 hours after a major rainstorm. The Surfrider Foundation puts out an annual "State of the Beach" report that can help you determine where it is and isn't safe.

3. Join a local chapter of the Surfrider Foundation, Surfers Environmental Alliance, or other ocean conservation groups working to protect local surf spots and improve beach water quality.

4. Insist that developers and government officials include surf and wave quality in their environmental impact assessments.

5. Respect those in the water with you, including marine animals. If you're surfing a popular beach, obey the rules on designated board surfing areas and times.

9. Fish for Fun, Food, and the Future

Responsible recreational fishing can
benefit ocean conservation.

Some 12 million Americans enjoy recreational saltwater fishing, according to the National Oceanic and Atmospheric Administration. They range from urban fishers taking their kids out on municipal piers to catch crappie, bass, and queenfish for dinner to the owners of powerful deep-sea fishing boats going after big blue-water gamefish such as marlin.

What these fishermen and women have in common is a multigenerational love of the sea and the sport. I remember my father taking my sister and me fishing on Sheepshead Bay, Brooklyn. It's one of those elemental experiences parents can pass on to their young that teaches about patience, reward, taking no more than your fair share, and baiting your own hook. The special nature of this experience is best summed up by the bumper sticker philosopher who claims, "A bad day fishing is better than a good day doing anything else."

Recreational fishermen and women were among the first to promote conservation of ocean fish and their habitat. The National Coalition for Marine Conservation was founded more than 30 years ago by conservation-minded fishermen. Working with other recreational fishing groups, it helped restore depleted striped bass populations along the East Coast in the 1980s (and continues today to fight for striper recovery). Recreational fishing groups have also lobbied for restrictions on commercial fishing when they felt that industry was damaging their shared resource.

Yet recreational fishers themselves don't always protect the environment they seek to enjoy. A 2004 study published in the journal *Science* suggested that the growing number of participants in the sport and increased use of high-tech fish-finding tools are harming some fish populations. A number of recreational fishing groups have also lobbied *against* the establishment of no-take underwater wilderness parks.

Still, people into fishing have a long history of working for marine conservation and careful management of our public fisheries. As more and more people are attracted to the sport, they have to continue educating themselves to protect both the fish and their home waters. Here's how you can fish responsibly:

1. Get a valid fishing license. License fees help pay for conservation and restoration and keep track of how many people are affecting the resource.

2. Follow fishing regulations. Obey season, size, and bag limits. You can get a copy of the rules when you buy your fishing license or at most bait and tackle shops.

3. Cooperate with the fish cops. Law enforcement agents have a tough job to do. They are there to protect both the resource and you.

4. Get involved in tag-and-release programs that help track fish populations. Follow instructions to return any tags you find.

5. If you're doing catch-and-release fishing, use barbless hooks, handle the fish gently when it's played out, and try not to remove it from the water; otherwise it's more likely to die once released.

6. Fish for species that are abundant, and avoid species that are overfished or poorly managed. Groups such as the National Coalition for Marine Conservation and cards listing sustainable seafood (see action 13) can help you make these determinations.

7. Make sure that any fishing tournaments you participate in have a strong conservation element. Read their literature and check them out with marine conservation groups before sending in your check.

10. Walk on Whatever Beach You Want

The beaches and sands along our shores are a birthright for all Americans to use, cherish, and protect.

"By the law of nature these things are common to all mankind: the air, running water, the sea, and consequently the shores of the sea." This law, established by Roman Emperor Justinian in A.D. 530, became, over the next millennium, the basis for English civil law and eventually for the United States law known as the public trust doctrine. This requires that American states (and territories) hold our beaches in trust for the benefit of all Americans to swim, fish, and otherwise enjoy without hindrance. The few exceptions are Massachusetts and Maine, where, back in the 1600s, colonial authorities sold off public land rights between the low and high tide marks to private interests, to raise funds to build shipping wharfs; a few "private" beaches; and military reserves. Other than those, most of the nation's beaches are open to all Americans. In Oregon, the public has the right to use the beach up to the line of vegetation where trees start growing behind the sand.

However, enforcing the public trust doctrine and providing public access to public beaches has become an ongoing battle between private developers, homeowners, and beachgoers from New Jersey to California. In northern New Jersey, the lack of public parking and access gates is a problem along an extensive taxpayer-built seawall. In Southern California a years-long battle between Hollywood celebrities living along the beach in Malibu and advocates of public access to the Pacific shore finally was resolved in 2005 in favor of the public.

Of course, when you visit the beach, be respectful of the rights of others. Behave in ways that improve rather than degrade the quality of the location and that help reduce tensions between oceanside owners and users, so that all can enjoy the beach. These are ways to do that:

1. Don't trespass onto or through private property on the landward side of a public beach. Look for public access signs.

2. Don't litter, play loud music, or otherwise disturb fellow beachgoers or the homeowners along the beach. Pack out everything you carry onto the sand.

3. Don't park illegally or in someone's private space when visiting the beach.

4. Be aware that hotels, beach clubs, and other private facilities that provide beach services (lifeguards, beach chairs, or the like) may ask you to pay a user fee on the beach adjoining them. These fees have usually been agreed upon by a state agency.

5. Find out whether the local townships charge a "reasonable" fee for use of public beaches and set beach rules such as no pets. Know the rules for the beaches you plan to visit.

6. Don't be intimidated if you're on the beach and someone tells you you're not allowed there. Know your rights, and politely explain the public trust doctrine, if necessary.

11. Talk about the Ocean in Your Place of Worship

The spiritual connection we feel with the ocean is a sacred trust.

Some of my greatest joys and sorrows have been associated with living by the sea, working and playing in the sea. Millions of people share this sense of connection to the ocean. After all, our bodies, like the planet, are 71 percent saltwater and our blood is as salty as the sea. It's no wonder it's so easy to sleep by the ocean. The sound of the waves is reminiscent of our mother's heartbeat. My late love often said I never looked happier than when I was coming out of the water after being beaten up by the waves. Every New Year's morning she'd insist we go to the ocean to start afresh.

Along with moments of transcendence and joy, the ocean can also provide solace, giving you a sense of being part of a larger whole, even when great parts of your own soul have been torn away. In looking from the tide pools to the stars, you can't help but recognize patterns of creation that reflect a profound sense of connectedness. This is the stuff of religion and of hope.

Increasingly our religious congregations, faiths, and leaders see that part of our spiritual duty is to act as guardians of the wonders of nature we've received and are meant to pass on. A few years ago I helped conduct a two-week training in environmental journalism for reporters from the region of the Black Sea. Our gathering was part of a larger meeting held in Turkey and sponsored by the Christian Orthodox Church that had developed in the area. The leader of the church declared that pollution and desecration of the Black Sea were sins. And couldn't the same be said of the destruction and pollution of the Gulf of Mexico, or of Prince William Sound, Alaska, or of countless other marine resources? Here are a few ways to preserve our sacred and life-affirming ocean:

1. In your place of worship, organize a youth outreach project to protect the sea, such as a beach cleanup (see action 27), water-quality testing, or storm-drain stenciling (see action 25).

2. Hold a spiritual or commemorative service by the ocean or by a waterway that flows to the sea.

3. Determine how your faith should guide you in taking actions for the coasts and ocean. Then discuss the role of water in your faith and how you and your congregation might better act to protect the world's waters.

4. Invite a marine conservation biologist from a local university or ocean group to your place of worship to discuss the relationship between faith and science.

5. Consider establishing an ecumenical project focused on the crisis faced by our world oceans.

section

2

. . . .

Conserve

12. Eat Organic and Vegetarian Foods

Understand the impact of your food choices on the sea.

Every year, farmers in the Midwest use as much as 140 pounds of synthetic fertilizer for every acre planted in corn and other chemical-dependent crops. Every spring, surplus fertilizer and other agricultural chemicals wash down the Mississippi River into the Gulf of Mexico where they encourage the growth of a massive algae bloom. When the algae decay they are fed on by bacteria, which suck the dissolved oxygen out of the water. The lack of oxygen creates a "dead zone" larger than New Jersey that kills every form of sea life that cannot flee its reaches.

Similar harmful algae blooms, dead zones, and diseases along our coasts are also linked to "nutrient" pollution from agricultural chemicals and factory farms. Concentrated animal feed operations for cattle, poultry, and hogs displace thousands of family farmers, crowd animals, and intensify pollution from animal wastes. At the same time factory farming offers little or no benefit in terms of the health and flavor of the meat and dairy products we consume. Much of the animal waste from these operations takes the form of nitrogen, which finds its way into our coastal waters, spreading diseases and smothering productive habitats such as sea grass meadows and coral reefs. Our food choices as consumers can significantly affect these trends. Simple things you can do include these:

1. Look for the organic label, and purchase organically grown foods whenever possible. This could significantly reduce the amount of chemical fertilizers flowing to the sea.

2. Choose a vegetarian diet or reduce the amount of meat you consume; you'll reduce the amount of water and waste required in the production of your food.

3. Try organic barley- or grass-fed beef as an alternative to corn-fed feedlot meat. Most American corn is grown with heavy applications of petrochemical fertilizers. What's more, cows' stomachs aren't adept at digesting corn, so its use as a primary feed has led to more sick animals, which generate more waste.

4. Try to purchase fresh, locally grown foods. Doing so reduces the amount of oil used to transport foods from fields to stores and also supports local farmers.

5. Let your retail grocer know that you prefer organic, locally grown, and sustainable foods, and support the brands, markets, farmers' markets, and restaurants that provide them.

6. Learn to savor the flavor: make fresh organic meals a center of your social and family life. Don't feel guilty about putting time into a fine meal. Treat your food as something more than fast fuel.

13. Eat Seafood That's Healthy and Sustainable

Eating the right fish protects your health; eating the wrong fish may leave the plate empty for the next generation.

Someone recently asked me if I still eat seafood. While I know that some of my professional peers disagree, I feel comfortable, in this fish-eat-fish world, eating any marine wildlife that's sustainable, meaning that it's not being caught faster than it can reproduce. That's not true of certain species of fish.

With a globalized seafood market, though, we often don't know the origins or environmental implications of what we're eating. People in San Francisco, for example, might unwittingly order shrimp from a polluted aquaculture farm in Ecuador, farmed salmon laden with antibiotics from Chile, or fish and chips containing fish caught by huge factory trawlers at sea—never realizing that these menu choices can be unhealthy for both themselves and the seas. Instead, those diners could have ordered wild salmon, Dungeness crabs and farmed oysters that are local, tasty, and abundant. Because local citizens, fishermen and women, and environmental groups have worked for years to clean up pollution off the coast of northern California, these dining choices are also healthy.

Unfortunately, seafood in other areas is not always healthy, even when it's sustainably managed. Many seafood products are contaminated with ocean pollutants such as mercury. Toxic chemicals dumped into the sea become concentrated as they work their way through the food web (as the big fish eat the little fish), so that top predators like tuna and swordfish are more likely to contain toxins such as mercury and PCBs than prey lower down the web, like sardines, anchovies, lobsters, and crabs.

To help consumers make choices that benefit both themselves and the living seas, a number of campaigns have recently emerged under the banner of the sustainable-seafood movement. One action encourages the labeling of healthy and sustainable seafood. Another educates concerned restaurant chefs through an organization called the Chefs Collaborative. Aquariums, conservation groups, and others have created citizen guides to sustainable seafood, printed on wallet-size cards. They suggest that people choose to eat wild Alaskan salmon, for example, rather than salmon from fish farms, whose wastes can pollute surrounding waters, or choose to order abundant species like calamari (squid) and Pacific halibut rather than overfished species such as orange roughy, grouper, and shark. Sustainable-seafood cards now incorporate human health concerns into their lists, with color-coded warnings about fish containing elevated levels of mercury, PCBs, and other pollutants.

Julie Packard, Director of the Monterey Bay Aquarium, explains that, "Overfishing is an environmental problem whose solution is in people's hands every time they buy seafood."

Pietro Parravano, a commercial fisherman from Half Moon Bay, California, and former president of the Pacific Coast Federation of Fishermen's Associations, agrees. "I think the consumer can play an increasingly important role helping fish, fishermen, and coastal communities."

Here are some ways to ensure that the seafood you consume, if you choose to do so, is healthy and sustainable:

1. Get a sustainable-seafood wallet guide, and carry it with you when you shop or go out to eat. Pass out extras to friends and co-workers. Aquariums and environmental groups, including the Monterey Bay Aquarium and Environmental Defense, distribute the cards free, and they can also be downloaded from the Internet.

2. Pick up one of several sustainable seafood cookbooks now available, including *One Fish, Two Fish, Crawfish, Bluefish: The Smithsonian Sustainable Seafood Cookbook* and *Seafood Lover's Almanac*.

3. Patronize stores and restaurants like Legal Sea Foods that support sustainable, healthy fisheries through Marine Stewardship Council labeling or membership in the Chefs Collaborative. A list of member restaurants can be found at www.chefscollaborative.org.

4. Complain to the managers of shops and restaurants that serve endangered fish items, such as West Coast rockfish and shark-fin soup, or fail to include health advisories for certain seafoods, such as swordfish and raw shellfish.

14. Grow a Natural Yard and Garden (and Play on a Natural Green)

What we plant can have a profound effect
on local waters that flow to the sea.

Along with agriculture, a major source of polluted runoff into our bays, estuaries, and coastal waters is urban runoff. Rainwater that flows over lawns and driveways carries large amounts of fertilizers, pesticides, oil, dirt, and other contaminants down storm drains and eventually into the sea. Golf courses, private lawns, and gardens often use more pesticides and fertilizers per acre than do many types of farming. Simple choices in how we maintain our yards and gardens can have profound effects on our local watersheds and coastal seas. If you love to garden, play a few rounds of golf on the weekend, or simply maintain green space around your home, the choices you make have profound impacts. Here are some basic guidelines:

1. Plant native trees, shrubs, flowers, and ground covers. In contrast to lawn turf, plants of varied heights absorb more rain and reduce erosion and runoff. Your local garden supply store or soil and water conservation agency can help you determine which native plants and shrubs are best for conserving water and reducing the need for chemical additives.

2. Create a rain garden—a shallow depression planted with perennials—to reduce runoff from your property.

3. Don't water every day. Twice a week is fine for most lawns and ground covers. When you water, irrigate slowly and deeply so that the water soaks into the soil rather then runs off it. It's better for the plants as well as for the oceans.

4. Set your mower blades high. Two to three inches is the proper height for most grasses to develop longer, healthier roots and ground shade. During droughts, leave your clippings on the grass to help retain moisture. In normal weather, compost the clippings to create mulch and natural fertilizer.

5. Keep your mower blades sharp, and vary the pattern you mow. This will reduce leaf damage, water loss, and soil compaction.

6. Test your soil for fertility, and plant accordingly. Use fertilizers sparingly, and never apply them before a heavy rainfall is forecast.

7. Use commonsense pest controls, including hand weeding, hand removal of insects, and encouragement of biological allies such as birds, bats, and ladybugs (learn how to attract them to your garden). Use pesticides only when pests increase beyond acceptable levels (if aphids are killing all your melons, lettuces, and beans for example), and then only sparingly.

8. If you hire professional lawn or landscape services, make sure they use methods and treatments that protect the environment, your health, and your watershed.

9. If you're a golfer, request that your golf club or the managers of the courses you play meet the standards of the United States Golf Association's Guide to Environmental Stewardship. These require reducing pesticide and herbicide use, reducing runoff, conserving water (and using reclaimed water for irrigation where possible), and protecting wetlands and woodlands.

15. Conserve Water

Water you save helps to keep clean rivers
flowing to the sea.

Water is the one substance on earth that naturally exists as a gas, a liquid, and a solid. The earth contains more than 330 million cubic miles of water. Of that, 96.5 percent is salt water in our global oceans. About another 1.75 percent is frozen in the polar icecaps and in glaciers, and 1.75 percent is found in rivers, lakes, streams, groundwater, and soil. Only .001 percent of the earth's water exists as vapor in the atmosphere (though having spent years living in the foggy regions of the San Francisco Bay I'd have guessed much more).

Climate change, driven by fossil fuel consumption, is increasing the frequency and severity of droughts, flooding, and other extreme weather events, which make fresh water less available. Growing population demands for fresh water are also beginning to strain water treatment, distribution, and disposal systems. Too much water diverted from rivers and streams will also reduce the amount of sand that accumulates on beaches, and impair the health of vitally important coastal wetlands and wildlife.

Even in areas with abundant water resources it makes sense to conserve water, because the less water flowing into local septic, sewage, and storm-drain systems, the better our waste facilities can process their loads and reduce polluted runoff into our bays and oceans. Conserving water also saves money and energy. Here's how you can help:

1. If your toilet was installed before 1992, add a toilet dam to reduce the amount of water flowing out of it by 35 percent and still leave it functioning properly. (Never use a brick to displace water in the tank, because it can deteriorate and clog your pipes.)

2. If possible, replace your old toilet with a modern low-flush one. While using only about half the water of old-style toilets, most newer models are now highly efficient.

3. Install a low-flow showerhead to reduce your shower water use by 20 to 60 percent.

4. Put aerators on all your faucets. They reduce the amount of water but add air bubbles so the flow remains lively. This way you can reduce your household water flow by two gallons a minute.

5. Check your pipes and water equipment for leaks, which can waste thousands of gallons of water a year.

6. Purchase water-saving appliances, such as a front-loading washing machine and low-water-use dishwasher, and wash only full loads.

7. Turn off the tap while brushing your teeth. Fill the basin for washing or shaving.

8. Wash fruits and vegetables in a bowl, and fill your sink to wash and rinse dishes, instead of running the water.

9. Landscape your property using native plants appropriate to your climate, so that they won't require excessive watering and will retain soil moisture.

10. Use a rain barrel to collect water from your roof's downspout to irrigate your garden.

11. Sweep, rather than spraying down, your driveway and sidewalk.

16. Conserve Energy to Help the Seas and Yourself

Energy conservation reduces the impact of power plants, which can poison ocean waters and fish.

Most power plants in the United States are still coal-fired. Coal is the oldest and most polluting fossil fuel used to generate electricity. Coal plants release both sulfur dioxide, which causes acid rain, and nitrogen oxide, which creates smog. Rain carries smog into bays and oceans, where it creates pollution and oxygen-depleted dead zones. Coal-generated power plants also release mercury, a neurotoxin that builds up in the flesh of top ocean predators such as tuna and swordfish, becoming a health risk for marine life and seafood consumers. In addition, burning coal adds a huge amount of climate-warming carbon dioxide to the atmosphere. Global warming, in turn, is changing the ocean's chemistry by making it more acidic and reducing its overall productivity.

While not as harmful as coal, other fossil fuel energies, including diesel oil and natural gas, also contribute to global warming and air and water pollution. We need to learn about and advocate for clean energy alternatives: wind, solar, biomass, geothermal, and tidal power, as well as hydrogen fuel cells for energy storage. To have an immediate impact in your daily life, you can reduce your "energy footprint" in ways that save both money and the sea.

1. Ask your utility provider for a free home energy audit. This will tell you ways you can save on your electric bill by eliminating wasted energy.

2. Properly insulate your home to save energy and money in both cold and hot weather. Install storm doors and windows, and weather-seal leaky windows.

3. If you can't afford double-pane windows, use window plastic from your hardware store to create a double layer. That extra pocket of insulating air will reduce heat loss 25 to 50 percent.

4. Turn off the lights and the television when you leave a room.

5. Replace incandescent lightbulbs with compact fluorescent bulbs. Although fluorescents are initially more expensive, they'll save you $60 over the course of the bulb's life.

6. Purchase EPA-rated "Energy Star" appliances, such as washers, dryers, air conditioners, and refrigerators. These energy-efficient models reduce pollution and greenhouse gas emissions by a third and can save about a third on your energy bill.

7. Look for the "Energy Star" rating when you purchase a new home.

8. Install a programmable thermostat that automatically adjusts your home temperature while you're away or asleep, to reduce your energy use. Wool sweaters, warm slippers,

and comforters can also help you keep the thermostat down in cold weather, and are way cozy.

9. Use an energy-efficient humidifier during the winter. According to the Department of Energy, moisture increases the "heat index," making 68 degrees feel like 76.

10. Install solar paneling and solar water-heating systems to save electricity.

11. In the winter, open your curtains and blinds during the day to let in solar radiation, and close them at night to keep the heat in. In the summer, reverse the process, keeping them closed during the day to keep the heat out.

12. Plant shade trees around your house, and encourage your city to plant and maintain an urban forest, reducing the need for fans and air-conditioning.

17. Be a Marine Sanctuary Volunteer

Our newest park system is largely underwater and in need of volunteers to help it grow and prosper.

The United States is blessed with 95,000 miles of coastline, which includes some of the finest coastal parks and marine reserves in the world. The National Marine Sanctuary system was created in 1972, 100 years after the dedication of Yellowstone as our first National Park. Today, there are 13 marine sanctuaries, including the historic shipwrecks of Thunder Bay in Lake Huron, the only sanctuary not on the ocean. A vast and remote stretch of island reefs and atolls north-west of Hawaii is slated to become the 14th sanctuary in the near future. This reserve extends more than 1,200 miles in length and contains 70 percent of the coral reefs of the United States. When dedicated, it will be seven times larger than the other 13 sanctuaries combined.

Three of today's largest sanctuaries, off California, Florida, and Massachusetts, were established in the wake of citizen protests against proposed offshore oil drilling in the 1980s.

While oil drilling and waste dumping are banned within sanctuary boundaries, other activities are permitted, including commercial and recreational fishing, shipping, and laying of communication cables. Many sanctuaries, from Texas to Georgia to Washington State, have broad support from both local citizens and visitors, including boaters, divers, and beachgoers. Citizen advisory councils and volunteer programs reflect this support. Programs such as the Farallones Marine Sanctuary Beach Watch train hundreds of volunteers to testify in court on oil spills, respond to marine mammal strandings, give beach profiles on deposits of sand and debris, tally bird and mammal populations, and watch and report on the natural cycles of the sea, among other activities. Here's how you can be a part of this dynamic new frontier:

1. Learn about your nearest (or favorite) marine sanctuary and about ocean and marine conservation on the Web sites of the sanctuary and conservation groups.

2. Contact local marine conservation organizations to learn about their views on sanctuary issues and their existing and needed programs.

3. Recruit friends and family who play on, work on, or enjoy the waters of marine sanctuaries to become involved in preserving them.

4. Call your local sanctuary office to find out about intern and summer work opportunities for students.

5. After discovering the sanctuaries, learn more about national parks and seashores, national wildlife refuges, and estuarine research reserves along our coasts, where you can also have fun, be inspired, and volunteer.

18. Prevent Sea Turtles from Going the Way of Dinosaurs

Taking simple actions and smart vacations can help protect these ancient wanderers.

Seven species of sea turtles have been swimming and grazing through the world's oceans for 120 million years. They are the descendants of giant land turtles that returned to the sea during the age of the dinosaurs. Unfortunately, today's sea turtle populations are threatened by a number of human activities. Hotels and houses on and near turtle nesting beaches have reduced their habitat, and artificial lighting disorients new hatchlings. Adult turtles are captured for eggs, meat, leather, and tortoiseshell, seriously reducing their population. They also die from ingesting plastic bags, balloons, and other garbage, drowning in fishing nets intended for other marine life, being injured by long-line fishing hooks, and becoming caught in shrimp trawls, to the point where several species, such as the Kemp's ridley and the leatherback, are on the brink of extinction. The female nesting population of leatherbacks, the largest of all sea turtles, has collapsed 95 percent since 1980.

Though protected under the Endangered Species Act, sea turtles continue to die in large numbers as a result of both commercial fishing operations and pollution of the seas. A global outbreak of unexplained tumors among sea turtles has affected their abilities to feed and function. A number of countries still allow the taking of sea turtles for meat or decorative uses, and, where this is forbidden, a black market often thrives.

Many efforts are being made to preserve sea turtles and restore them to healthy populations. Advocates fight to protect nesting beaches in the United States. A growing number of countries, such as Mexico, Cuba, and Costa Rica, have introduced turtle excluder devices (TEDs) on shrimp trawl nets. Safer "round" hooks have been introduced on long-line fishing vessels. In areas where there is a high risk to endangered turtles, certain fishing vessels have been banned. Conservation groups such as the Sea Turtle Restoration Project work directly with fishing groups and go to court when necessary to see these reforms implemented. Here are some ways you can help save sea turtles:

1. Refrain from driving on or setting campfires on turtle nesting beaches in Florida, Texas, and elsewhere. During nesting season, refrain from walking on these beaches at night.

2. Keep bright lights from shining on nesting beaches. A number of local communities turn off their ocean-facing lights during nesting season. Use light shields for house and street lamps.

3. Never release helium balloons into the air or dump plastic bags in the ocean; these materials resemble jellyfish, sea turtles' favorite food, and can cause turtles to choke and die.

4. If you're snorkeling, don't grab or try to catch a ride on a sea turtle. They breathe above water and can be seriously

stressed by being held under water. If you don't thrash around in the water, most turtles will go about their business so that you can watch them feed and interact with each other.

5. If you see anyone harassing a sea turtle or poaching a nest, report the abuse to the local police or marine patrol.

6. Don't shell out for illegal sea turtle products, such as tortoiseshell combs or jewelry, and don't eat turtle eggs, steaks, or soup when you're traveling overseas.

7. Choose ecotourism destinations where sea turtles and other ocean resources are protected. How you spend your dollars can be a powerful argument for conservation. Groups such as the International Ecotourism Society can help you discover whether your vacation destination is a place where protecting the marine environment is taken seriously.

19. Use Less Plastic

The plastic that finds its way into the ocean
never stops polluting.

Plastic food wrappers, bags, balloons, bottles, cigarette filters and packaging, monofilament fishing nets and line, Styrofoam pellets, and other objects make up about 60 percent of the trash found on beaches and about 90 percent of the debris found floating in the world's oceans.

Bits of plastic are absorbed or eaten by jellyfish, finned fish, turtles, birds, marine mammals, and other creatures, who mistake the pieces for food. Stranded seals and turtles have been found with their stomachs so full of plastic that they are unable to feed and are starving. Seabirds that mistake plastic pellets for food feed them to their chicks. After a major retail chain store opened on St. Thomas in the U.S. Virgin Islands, I noticed that the ferry channel between St. Thomas and nearby St. John was littered with floating bags from that store. Plastic fish nets and cargo strapping entangle sea lions and other creatures, slowly strangling them as they grow larger. Plastic "ghost nets" discarded or lost at sea from fishing boats continue to ensnare and kill marine wildlife, sinking with the weight of

54

their kill until gases formed by the decaying animals float the nets back up to kill again. Unlike cotton fishing nets, these nets never dissolve.

While oil spills are a terrible environmental threat, oil is not nearly as destructive as the accumulation of everyday plastic items; oil eventually biodegrades, but plastic lasts forever. Through a process called *photo degradation,* sunlight slowly breaks down plastic polymers into pellets and fine dust. A study by the Algalita Marine Research Foundation found that plastic dust in parts of the North Pacific Ocean weighs six times more than zooplankton, the tiny animals that form the base of the marine food web. Marine plastic also acts as a toxic sponge, absorbing pollutants in the water such as PCBs and DDT. It concentrates these poisons tens of thousands of times more than seawater can. When consumed by fish, this poisonous plastic dust becomes part of the food web, increasing the toxic load in the flesh of tuna, billfish, sharks, and other top predators that humans then consume. Studies are now underway to see how these toxic loads may affect the development and reproduction of marine animals.

Researchers who've been tracking marine debris believe plastic in the ocean may be one of the most alarming and least known environmental stories of our time.

An international dumping treaty prohibits all overboard disposal of plastics from ships and boats, but the greatest "pulse" of plastic debris into the ocean comes from land-based human activities, particularly our habit of discarding plastic packaging material, plastic water bottles, and plastic toys. Even plastic bags thrown in the trash and taken to the landfill may be carried by the breeze back out to sea.

At the end of World War Two, plastic was a new creation that, like rayon, was seen as a way to reduce our dependence on foreign sources of rubber and silk. Today every American tosses out about 65 pounds of plastic a year. By reducing demand for plastic and limiting its use to essential purposes we can help save the greater part of our blue planet. Here's how you can do your part:

1. Secure any plastic you bring onboard a boat or to the beach. Make sure the plastic you bring, whether a waterproof bag, rain slicker, or beach bucket goes home with you.

2. Dispose properly of cigarette packaging and butts with plastic filters. Throwing them on the beach or at the curb will likely take them out to sea by way of the tides, winds, and storm drains.

3. Recycle plastic when you can. Studies show less than 5 percent of plastic ever gets recycled. Some plastics can't be recycled because of their chemical makeup. While the plastic industry uses a numbering system to group plastics into seven categories, only #1 PET and #2 HDPE narrow-necked bottles are commonly recycled into new material. Some communities collect all seven kinds of plastic and then throw out everything but #1 and #2.

4. Bring cloth bags from home for your groceries or other purchases. The plastic bags used at the checkout stand are not recyclable and could end up killing marine wildlife.

5. When you move to a new home, use materials such as real popcorn or newspapers for packing rather than Styrofoam peanuts. If you receive Styrofoam peanuts and bubble wrap in packaging sent to you, take them to a packaging store that accepts them for reuse.

6. Buy products that are recycled and reusable. Avoid throwaway items such as plastic forks, cups, and water bottles.

7. Buy products with less packaging. Buying from bulk bins can reduce waste and save money. Avoid bulk products that have individually wrapped items within them.

8. At retail outlets where you shop, look and ask for new biodegradable "green plastics" made of agricultural materials such as cornstarch.

9. As you reduce your dependence on plastic, encourage friends and family to do the same, and tell them the reasons behind your actions.

20. Opt Out of the Throwaway Culture

What we throw out doesn't ever really go away.

My cousin's husband Mark recently complained to me when their new toaster broke down. It was designed, he noted, in a way that made it difficult to open and repair, likely so that the average consumer would give up and buy a new one. (He managed to fix it, but it took persistence.) I certainly remember seeing a lot more repair shops when I was growing up than I find now, for shoes, typewriters, and small appliances. When something broke, people didn't automatically throw it away.

By creating a throwaway culture, we condemn ourselves to using more energy to manufacture and transport products (which translates into more fossil fuel burned and more airborne pollutants deposited in the sea), accumulating more junk (and plastic packaging) that can make its way to the sea, and reducing self-sufficiency (which makes us more passive and less willing to do something that might actually benefit our blue planet).

The links between today's use-once-and-dump consumer lifestyle and the health of the environment aren't always clear and apparent. But it is clear that by consuming less, or consuming less harmful products, you can have a direct impact on the health of the waters you depend on and the fish and marine products you make use of. And by changing your lifestyle, you can also begin to change your identity from passive consumer to active citizen.

1. Focus on the things you and your family value and love that aren't consumer products (going to the beach, for example) and focus on "having more fun" as an alternative to "buying more stuff."

2. When looking for a home, try to locate in an area where shops, parks, and other amenities are close enough so that you don't have to drive to them (or drive the kids).

3. Look for additional opportunities to walk, bike, or otherwise reduce your dependence on fossil fuels.

4. Prepare more (and healthier) meals at home. Save dining out for special occasions. Just think of the fuel, money, and time you will save.

5. Repair, reuse, and recycle the things you own. Thrift was once an American value and should be again. Groups such as the Center for a New American Dream are working to promote this idea.

6. Make "funky chic" your fashion statement. Why can't you be both stylish and practical with hand-me-downs, thrift store bargains, and found items?

7. Simplify the holidays and add meaning to them by giving ocean-friendly gifts and spending more time with the people you love.

21. Raise Funds for Ocean Conservation

Buying an ocean-friendly license plate or baking cookies for a fundraiser can help support ocean conservation.

In Florida you can get license plates that support manatees, sea turtles, or coral reefs. In California, whale tail license plates help support coastal protection. In Virginia a plate benefits the local Surfrider Foundation, a group of wave-riding ecoactivists. State drivers pay extra for these specialty license plates to show their commitment to ocean conservation. Beyond providing much-needed funds, the plates also remind fellow drivers about environmental perils and perhaps inspire them to support conservation efforts.

You can participate in or plan a great many fun and helpful fundraising activites—from bake sales to T-shirt sales and calendar sales, from silent auctions to seaside dinners and sunset cruises. Reef Relief's annual Cayo Carnival draws thousands of people to the old fort in Key West for food, drink, and live music in a town that knows how to party for a cause. Whether you're donating a few dollars online or spearheading a fund drive on behalf of your favorite marine conservation organization, helping to pay the cost of protecting and restoring our living seas is an investment guaranteed to provide long-term benefits. Here's how to begin:

1. If you're thinking of contributing money, consider dividing it between a small marine group that's fighting to protect a local resource and a regional or national group that's addressing the same issue on a broader scale.

2. Ask friends, co-workers, and your employer if they'll match your contribution. Even $20 or $100 each can really add up.

3. Find out if the group you're interested in is seeking in-kind support. Its staff might need office equipment that you have, a couple of hours of volunteer time per week, or something more creative.

4. Offer your skills or resources to the cause. If you work in advertising, perhaps you can help on an educational campaign. If you own a boat, you might offer a day on the water as a great silent auction gift.

5. Give your suggestions and help for fundraising festivals, beach parties, regattas, and other special events. These can prove especially useful not only for fundraising but also for recruiting advocates and educating new people about the group's work.

6. Reach out to local businesses, foundations, and ocean-dependent enterprises for help. It's surprising where you'll find unexpected friends and supporters.

3

Clean

22. Maintain an Ocean-Friendly Driveway or Green Roof

Create surfaces that help rainwater soak back into the earth and reduce pollution.

A number of scientific studies have found that water quality begins to deteriorate when more than 10 percent of a coastal watershed is covered in impermeable surfaces (hard layers such as pavement and concrete that rainwater can't percolate through). Waters that run off hard surfaces like pavement do not have the opportunity to soak back into the earth. Instead of being absorbed and filtered through the soil, the rainwater pools and floods, picking up debris, oily wastes, and other contaminants and depositing them in local waterways. Driveways, roofs, and sidewalks are major sources of this type of urban runoff. One inch of rainfall on the typical home's driveway produces approximately 900 gallons of runoff water that enters local storm drains and finds its way to the sea. One way to reduce this runoff is to build a more permeable driveway for your home.

Another way is to build a green roof. In Europe, it's not unusual to see home and apartment roofs covered in soil and plants to make them more absorbent, energy-efficient, and attractive. Green roofs reduce the accumulation of heat in urban areas, increase urban greenery, and decrease storm-water runoff. In the United States, the idea of green roofs is newer, used mainly on commercial and industrial buildings so far, One is Ford's Dearborn Michigan Truck Plant, at 454,000 square feet the largest green roof in the world. It can absorb almost 500,000 gallons of rainwater, saving the company $10 million a year it would otherwise spend for storm-water treatment. Of course, individuals need to make changes at a smaller scale than that. Here are a few ways to get started:

1. Instead of paving your driveway, use gravel, crushed seashells, or woodchips. That's the easiest way to reduce your runoff.

2. If you still opt for a hard surface driveway, install widely spaced concrete slabs or bricks, and fill the gaps with sand or grass.

3. Choose paving blocks called "permeable pavers," which look like ordinary cobblestones or bricks but have channels that funnel water between the blocks, allowing it to percolate into the ground.

4. Consider installing a green roof. Most start with a water-proof lining that is then covered with thin layers of soil and vegetation. The Web site www.Greenroofs.com can steer you to local contractors and others familiar with proper construction techniques.

5. Use native plants for your green roof cover. They are better adapted to grow well and to weather seasonal changes in your area. After an initial period of watering and fertilizing, green roofs are surprisingly low-maintenance and very attractive.

23. Keep Your Household Refuse Nontoxic

Chemicals tossed in the garbage find their way into streams, rivers, and eventually the sea.

Many household cleaning products contain toxic chemicals. So do some types of carpeting, insulation, maintenance materials, and construction materials. Batteries, thermostats with mercury switches, computers containing lead, and other electronic household products are particularly hazardous. Lead, mercury, and other persistent organic pollutants (POPs) can build up or "bio-accumulate" in the food chain. Small amounts of these chemicals tossed into the garbage eventually leach out of landfills and into the planet's water system. There they concentrate in plankton, which feed small baitfish, which in turn feed larger predator fish, which are consumed by humans, bears, and marine mammals. As a result, creatures such as beluga whales and polar bears have been found with extremely high concentrations of synthetic chemicals in their body fat. Certain top-of-the-food-web predator fish and many fish caught in urban harbors have become a health risk to consumers, particularly children, pregnant women, and people with medical problems.

Chemical and heavy metal wastes have been linked to increased risks of cancer, birth defects, developmental deficits, and neurological diseases. Much of this "circle of poison" could be eliminated if we'd just begin to replace the toxic chemicals around us with benign and nontoxic alternatives. Here's how you can help stop the cycle:

1. Remove your shoes when you enter your house, to avoid tracking in harmful amounts of pesticides, lead, and other contaminants. Keep a welcome mat at the door for people to wipe their feet on before they enter your home. There's already enough bad stuff in your house that you want to clear out without tramping more in.

2. Use baking soda, vinegar, lemon juice, and water for cleaning a range of items, including ovens, windows, kitchen counters, and mirrors, instead of using more harmful (and expensive) cleaning agents. Baking soda also freshens drains.

3. Substitute cedar chips for toxin-heavy mothballs.

4. Keep herbal mixtures or lemon, vinegar, and water in spray pump bottles to use in place of air fresheners containing potentially harmful chemicals.

5. Choose carpets with nontoxic backings and "green" building materials. These are now widely available at competitive prices.

6. Never throw household batteries, computers, television sets, and other appliances containing harmful components into the trash. Instead dispose of them through your local recycling center. Many drugstores, office-supply stores, and other retail outlets now accept batteries and printer cartridges for recycling.

24. Drive a Fuel-Efficient Car, Join a Car Pool, or Use Public Transit

Tailpipe emissions are a major source of ocean pollution.

Our coastal waters are poisoned not only from land-based runoff but also from airborne deposits of nitrogen oxide, a tailpipe pollutant that may account for more than 25 percent of the nitrogen buildup in offshore waters. Nitrogen feeds algae blooms that result in oxygen-depleted dead zones offshore. American cars, trucks, and SUVs also contribute a major proportion of the world's carbon dioxide emissions, a key factor in global warming. American vehicles alone produce more greenhouse gases than are produced by any single nation except China.

Fossil-fuel-driven climate change is already affecting the ocean—increasing water levels, water temperatures, water acidity, erosion, and storm surges. It is also bleaching and killing corals. While it will be some time before we have pollution-free means of transportation (other than bikes and feet), it makes sense to drive more fuel-efficient vehicles today and to maintain them in ways that reduce their fuel consumption. Here's how you can do this:

1. Buy a hybrid car. Gas/electric vehicles like the midsize Toyota Prius are rated to get around 50 miles per gallon on the highway and 60 in the city. They get better mileage in the city because that's where drivers are likely to do more stop-and-go driving. Hybrids recover energy during braking and idling, and use it to charge their batteries; they don't need to be plugged in to recharge.

2. Walk or bike for short errands.

3. If possible, carpool or take public transportation to commute to work. Internet sites such as eRideShare.com link compatible carpoolers ("nonsmoker, radio sports fan looking for van buddies").

4. If you live in a town with a good public transit system, such as San Francisco, New York, or Washington, consider not owning a car. You can always rent one if you need to, or;

5. Join a car-share program such as Zipcar, which allows you to rent a car by the hour if you're only an occasional driver. Many cities now have this innovative form of vehicle sharing. Go to www.carsharing.net to see if your town does.

6. Maintain your vehicle properly, with regular oil changes and tune-ups, to dramatically increase vehicle life and reduce emissions.

7. Keep your tires fully inflated, to increase your fuel efficiency and reduce emissions.

8. Do your automotive business, including car buying, with companies that show a commitment to the highest environmental standards.

25. Don't Use Your Storm Drain as If It Were a Toilet

What goes down the storm drain soon finds
its way to the sea.

Storm drains flush excess waters from rainstorms, snow-storms, and hurricanes into nearby rivers and bays or directly into the sea. People often think that storm drains lead to their local water treatment plant, but most do not. In Los Angeles, former director of sanitation Judy Wilson calls the first rains of winter, "the first flush." She explains, "That's when all the paper, plastic, and everything else collected in the storm drains just gets whooshed down to the ocean, and you get tons of trash on the beach, along with oil and grease that's collected on the freeways during the dry season, and also your dog poop, the chemicals used on your lawn, and everything people use to wash their cars."

Storm-drain pollutants not only harm the seas but also harm beachgoers and marine life. A study in Los Angeles found that people swimming within 500 feet of storm-drain outlets had a 57 percent greater chance of getting sick than those who kept a greater distance away. One of every 25 people swimming near the outlets got sick with pollution-related illnesses or infections.

Some cities have begun to divert part of their storm water to sewage plants for treatment before releasing it into the sea. Others are installing more sophisticated filters on storm drains. Unfortunately, a number of cities, including Washington, that have combined their sewage and storm-drain systems find that their waste-treatment plants overflow during heavy rains, adding untreated sewage to the storm water released into local waters.

One obvious way to reduce storm water pollution is to make sure that nothing but rainwater goes down your storm drains in the first place. Here are some ways to do this:

1. Throw all trash in garbage cans. Don't drop gum, paper, cigarette butts, or other waste down a storm-drain grating or even on the pavement.

2. Use soap sparingly when washing your car.

3. Use a broom to sweep your driveway rather than watering it down, and put everything you sweep up into a garbage can.

4. If you use chemicals on your lawn, don't spray them on a windy day (so that they blow into waterways) or just before rain is predicted (so that they are carried away by runoff). Better yet, learn how to maintain your lawn and garden without chemicals (see action 14).

5. Control erosion from your property by planting ground cover, especially native plants, to secure the soil.

6. Don't change your oil in your driveway, and never dump oil or oily wastes on the street or down a storm drain. Recycle your oil, and immediately fix any oil leaks in your car. One gallon of oil can pollute 250,000 gallons of seawater.

7. When you walk your pet, scoop up the waste and dispose of it in a garbage can. Some 15 tons of pet wastes end up in our oceans every day, adding pathogens and bacteria that can sicken both marine animals and people.

8. Join a storm-drain stenciling project. Students and volunteers paint images of fish or dolphins and warnings such as 'No Dumping! Flows to Sea' at storm-drain inlets. Project sponsors include cities, water districts, and activist groups. If your city doesn't have a stencil project, encourage it to start one.

9. If you see someone dumping litter or waste down a storm drain, offer to help them dispose of the waste in a more environmentally friendly way, and explain why that's so important.

26. Upgrade Your House above Hurricane Code

**We can all learn from the lesson of "The Three Little Pigs":
build your house to withstand disaster.**

Howling winds, driving rains, eroding sands, mudslides, coastal fires, pounding hurricanes, and periodic earthquakes are all part of the natural cycle of the shore, which is why, throughout most of human history, people chose to live some distance inland.

Nobody should be encouraged to build in harm's way, but if you already live by the shore or are rebuilding there, do the necessary research and invest in the proper precautions to protect your property. Your actions can spell the difference between minor landscaping damage and total devastation. By building tough, you'll not only spare your house but also spare the beach and ocean from the piles of wreckage, plastic, propane, automobiles, and other debris left in the wake of hurricanes.

Strong foundations and (in zones that frequently flood) elevation are two key elements for securing coastal homes and businesses. Building a house on concrete pillars that go to bedrock may sound extreme, but when all the sand washes out to sea, such a house will still be standing. The Federal Emergency Management Agency (FEMA) and certain states require some homes be built 12 to 14 feet above the ground. Elevation works, provided the raised home is also secure enough to withstand strong winds and other damaging forces (such as heavy debris) often linked to hurricane flooding. A number of actions strengthen a home against coastal storm impacts, just as many of California's structures have been retrofitted to protect against earthquakes. Here are a few:

1. After building a strong foundation, install threaded rods that go up through the framing to the rafters. These act as the bones of the structure.

2. Reinforce interior walls. They will resist twisting when a house is hit by strong winds.

3. Get the best windows and doors you can afford that include impact-resistant glass and a layer of shatterproof laminate.

4. Install storm-rated hurricane shutters.

5. Use clips and connectors to fortify floors, walls, rafters, and roofs.

6. Install a metal roof. These roofs have proved durable in hurricane-force winds. They also save energy and resist fire.

7. Consider using low-maintenance composite decking and fiber-cement siding. Both perform well in storms and flooding.

8. Consider buying a generator. In storm zones, this may be a worthwhile investment. During the 2004 and 2005 hurricane seasons some communities went without power for weeks.

27. Join in a Coastal Cleanup

Protect the shoreline while getting some healthy
outdoor exercise.

Beach cleanups and Adopt-a-Beach programs are great ways
to protect the marine environment and popular recreational sites while getting exercise in beautiful settings. The amount
and types of trash found reveal the impact of our consume-and-
discard culture. On a state beach in isolated Wallis, New
Hampshire, for example, volunteers collected 350 pounds of
trash on a single day in December 2004.

The most common trash items found (80 percent) are cigarette butts and filters, food wrappers and containers, caps and
lids, plastic bags and bottles, glass bottles, plastic eating uten-
sils, cans, straws, and tobacco packaging. Among items of
particular danger to marine wildlife are balloons, plastic bags,
fishing line, fishing nets, plastic rope, plastic six-pack holders,
abandoned fish traps, and syringes. More than 800,000 of these
items were found during one year's International Coastal
Cleanup Day. Other items found ranged from truck tires to
refrigerators to toilets and, yes, to kitchen sinks.

In 1986 the Center for Marine Conservation (now known as the Ocean Conservancy) began the International Coastal Cleanup that takes place every September. Close to half a million participants worldwide now clear hundreds of tons of trash from coastlines, rivers, and lakes. Sponsors of local beach cleanups include state agencies such as the California Coastal Commission, major corporations, municipalities, and marine conservation groups. Here are things to remember if you'd like to participate:

1. When joining a beach cleanup, make sure you follow the instructions of the beach captain and sign a liability waiver.

2. Wear gloves (at least one), closed-toe shoes, protective clothing, and sunblock.

3. Pick up even small items of trash (like cigarette filters and bits of Styrofoam), which animals often mistake for food.

4. Do not pick up dead animals or attempt to move an injured animal. Call the beach captain or a lifeguard.

5. Do not pick up syringes, needles, sharp objects, weapons, or items containing human blood or fluids. Mark the site with sticks or stones, and notify the beach captain.

6. Leave undisturbed natural items such as kelp, driftwood, and shell fragments.

7. Fill out the data cards you're given. The information volunteers collect is used to help identify sources of pollution and create disposal policies that reduce the amounts of garbage that end up on our beaches and in our waters.

8. Consider becoming a sponsor or getting your business, community group, or place of worship to sponsor a local beach cleanup.

28. Protect Our Waters from Invasive Organisms (Exotic Critters)

One of the greatest rapidly growing threats to our waters is the introduction of non-native plants, animals, and microorganisms.

Invasive aquatic species have taken up residence in United States waters and have eaten, displaced, spread disease to, or otherwise threatened native creatures and their habitats. In the San Francisco Bay, one of the most damaged areas, with more than 130 invasive species, a new species is introduced every 14 weeks, threatening the survival of an entire native ecosystem.

Most invasive creatures are released from commercial ships' ballast waters. Large ships take in water for stability before a voyage and then release this ballast water when they reach their port of destination. Every hour of every day some 2 million gallons of ballast water are released in United States ports, harbors, and bays. Unfortunately, along with water, sand,

and rocks, this ballast carries some 3,000 foreign marine species, from plankton to clams to predator fish. The Environmental Protection Agency, the coast guard, and other government agencies are attempting to regulate ballast waters to reduce or eliminate the introduction of invasive species.

But commercial ships aren't the only contributors to this problem; small boat operators, fishermen, divers, pet owners, aquarium owners, travelers, and even seafood lovers also introduce invasive species into our marine waters. Pythons and giant monitor lizards have recently shown up in Florida's everglades, and lionfish with poisonous quills (native to the tropical Pacific) have appeared in Florida's ocean waters; these exotic pets were either released into the wild by their owners when they grew too large or troublesome or escaped unintentionally because the owners lacked proper education on pet care.

Exotic invasions also occur when people dump plants, algae, or even empty shells, which may contain living larvae, into bodies of water that did not harbor them before. Something as innocuous as an outboard motor or scuba tank, if not properly washed first, could transport an invasive species when it is moved from one ocean to another.

Here's how you can help reduce this problem:

1. When disassembling your aquarium, give the fish and invertebrates away, or return them to your pet store. Then place any unwanted plants, gravel, and other aquarium materials in a paper bag, and dispose of them in the trash.

2. Bag unused fishing bait and bait-packing material, and dispose of it in the garbage; do not release it in the water. Many bait worms and even some of the vegetation they're packed in are exotic species imported from Southeast Asia.

3. After that delicious seafood feast, don't dump oyster shells or other shellfish or seafood waste in the water. They may contain live "spat" (shellfish larvae), pathogens, and parasites.

4. Thoroughly clean your boat hull, trailer, anchor, fishing gear, scuba gear, mask, snorkel, and other sporting equipment before going from one major body of water to another.

5. Join local efforts to spot and remove invasive species. Support national efforts by ocean conservation groups, the coast guard, port authorities, and others to control ballast discharges.

6. Don't flush kitty litter down the toilet. Cat feces contain Toxoplasma, a genus of deadly pathogens that, along with opossum droppings, have been found to be one of the causes of sea otter deaths off the California coast. Kitty litter will also clog your toilet.

29. Sail on an Ocean-Friendly Cruise Ship

Avoid vacationing on a floating source of pollution.

While ocean liners were once the major transportation for people crossing oceans to work and emigrate, today most people fly, and the old steam liners have been replaced by a new generation of cruise ships built for fun. More than 200 modern cruise ships now carry more than 10 million vacationers on the world's oceans every year, including more than 7 million United States residents, according to industry statistics. These floating vacation palaces, some carrying more people than an aircraft carrier, can be found in every ocean environment from the Arctic seas to the coral reefs of the Tropics. As the primary customers of an industry expected to double its passenger load by 2010, American passengers can play a significant role in making sure the ships celebrate the sea and don't pollute it.

A typical 3,000-passenger cruise ship on a one-week voyage generates one million gallons of "gray water" (from sinks, showers, and laundries); more than 200,000 gallons of sewage; 25,000 gallons of oily bilge water; more than 100 gallons of hazardous waste (from dry cleaning, photo processing, and other chemical activities); 50 tons of garbage (plastic, paper, cardboard, food, and glass); and as much diesel exhaust as several thousand cars. Such a ship also contributes to the spread of invasive species from pumped out bilge water (see action 28).

Passengers often believe that the ship's waste is treated or stored for land removal, but in fact most of it is dumped at sea, sometimes illegally. One of the worst impacts of cruise ships may be their discharge of nutrient-rich sewage around coral reefs that thrive in a low-nutrient environment; this destructive method of sewage disposal encourages the growth of algae, which in turn smother and kill coral reefs.

Things can and must change. In 2004, Royal Caribbean pledged to install advanced wastewater treatment systems on its entire 28-ship fleet within the next 15 years. A small number of cruise ships also use gas-turbine engines that reduce harmful air pollutants by up to 90 percent. Alaska, Maine, and California have passed laws restricting sewage dumping in their waters, and a national Clean Cruise Ship bill to set higher environmental standards for the industry has been introduced in Congress. Several ocean conservation groups, such as Oceana and Blue Water Network (see Resources), are conducting public education campaigns to help reform the industry. But the greatest force for change can be the millions of Americans who are more than 70 percent of the industry's customers. Here's how to be a responsible cruise passenger:

1. If you're planning a cruise, investigate the cruise line to make sure its ships don't have a record of pollution. While the coast guard maintains these records, it may be easier to access them through a conservation group such as Blue Water Network. Let your booking agent know that this is a priority of yours.

2. Document any dumping that you observe while on a cruise by taking pictures or video footage. If it involves plastic or hazardous materials contact the coast guard's National Response Center (see Resources).

3. If you are uncertain of the contents of the wastes you document being dumped or pumped, complain to the cruise ship company, and contact a marine conservation group that works on cruise ship pollution issues.

4. Talk to your friends, neighbors, and fellow passengers about how cruise ships can be cleaner and greener (or "bluer").

5. Ask your congressional representative and senators to support the Clean Cruise Ship Act. You can identify and contact your member online at www.house.gov/writerep or senator at www.senate.gov.

section

4

....

Protect

30. Support Your Local Wetlands

Swamps are the filters, shelters, and nurseries of the sea;
they are also highly effective storm barriers.

For generations, coastal wetlands were perceived as dank and dangerous swamps, home to snakes, alligators, and the occasional philosophical opossum (as in the old comic strip *Pogo*). Since World War Two, more than 50 million acres of farmland have been paved over by urban and suburban development, while more than 53 million acres of wetlands have been filled in for agricultural use. Millions more acres of coastal wetlands have been replaced by housing developments, hotels, roads, and other construction, as more and more people move to the coasts. These activities were considered reasonable trade-offs until science began identifying wetlands as a key habitat for migratory birds and wildlife, a nursery for 75 percent of our marine fisheries, a filtration system for pollution, a recharger of subterranean aquafers, and a protective barrier against damage from coastal storms and hurricanes.

Flying over the bayou of coastal Louisiana, I've seen shredding islands of brown spartina or salt grass crosshatched both with canals built by oil companies to access their near shore drilling facilities and with massive flood control channels and levees built by the U.S. Army Corps of Engineers. Traditionally, flooding by the Mississippi River deposited sediment that built up the delta, but now sediment is flushed out into the deep Gulf of Mexico by these aquatic speedways. Meanwhile, oil drilling has caused land subsidence, and climate change has brought a rise in the sea level. Combined, these factors have shrunk the wetlands by some 35 square miles a year in recent decades.

Even when it was built in 1718, New Orleans was at some risk of flooding, but it had more than 150 miles of protective wetlands between itself and the Gulf. Every few miles of buffering wetlands reduce hurricane storm surges by a foot. But when Hurricane Katrina veered to the east of the city in late August 2005, there were not even 30 miles of wetlands buffer left in that direction. Other towns devastated by that hurricane, such as Biloxi, Mississippi, had filled in their salt marshes with waterfront casinos that drew thousands of new job-seeking residents to settle in harm's way.

In addition to acting as storm barriers, coastal wetlands, salt marshes, and estuaries often trail off into sea grass meadows that secure the nearshore bottom, reduce turbidity, and provide vital habitat for juvenile fish and shellfish. Unfortunately, despite some recent protections, more than half of United States wetlands have been destroyed by development. More than 95 percent of California's wetlands have been lost. Protection, appreciation, and physical restoration of our coastal wetlands are projects now being undertaken at many scales, from neighborhood-sponsored cleanups and plantings on the edges of Chesapeake Bay to multibillion-dollar efforts carried out by state and federal agencies to restore the Florida Everglades and the Louisiana Bayou wetlands, the latter project barely underway when Katrina struck. Robust, revitalized wetlands could still greatly alleviate future storm impacts.

If restoring wetlands feels like a daunting task, consider this: each of these efforts began with the concern of individual citizens such as Marjory Stoneman Douglas, whose 1947 book *The Everglades: River of Grass* described this natural treasure. As founder of Friends of the Everglades, she was a leading champion of her "river," continuing her crusade until her death in 1998 at the age of 108. All across the United States, people just like her continue to work for the wetlands and coastal "swamps" they love and value. Here's how you can do the same:

1. Turn to organizations such as Restore America's Estuaries and the National Oceanic and Atmospheric Administration (NOAA) to find out if there is a local watershed group involved in the protection of wetlands in your area. If so, volunteer or donate to its efforts.

2. If no such a group operates in your area, start one with friends and neighbors. Begin by educating yourselves: contact some of the wetlands groups listed in the Resources directory at the end of this book, and set some clear goals for what you'd like to achieve.

3. Buy a federal duck stamp at your local post office; though not valid for postage, duck stamps act as a hunting license, an admission to national wildlife sanctuary, and are popular among collectors. 98 percent of its price ($15 per stamp) goes to purchase wetlands and other vital habitat for waterfowl.

4. Learn about ways to increase tidal flow in blocked areas, plant native plants, and carry out other improvements to degraded wetlands in your area. Groups such as the Waterkeeper Alliance, local university coastal science programs, and watershed groups can help you find this information.

5. If you launch your own efforts to restore wetlands, coasts, and streams, apply for grants or technical assistance from NOAA, the federal Fish and Wildlife Service, and other government agencies that can provide help.

31. Restore a Stream, River, or Watershed

Healthy, flowing waters help assure thriving
coasts and oceans.

Water is in a constant flow from the sea to the sky, through evaporation, to the mountains; through precipitation as rain, sleet, and snow; and then back to the sea, following gravity in the world's streams and rivers. Even if you don't live anywhere close to the sea, you are probably within a marine watershed, the landscape through which water flows to the sea. The Mississippi River watershed that drains into the Gulf of Mexico covers 41 percent of the continental United States and more than half its farmland. Chesapeake Bay's watershed spreads through six states and the District of Columbia. Other major watersheds flowing into America's seas include those of the Yukon and Columbia Rivers, Mobile Bay, and the Hudson River. Constructing buildings, hard surfaces, storm drains, dams, artificial flood-control channels, or other alterations in watersheds can affect the amount and quality of groundwater and river water running through them, often decreasing the flow and increasing the pollution. During much of the year, the water of the Los Angeles River, encased in concrete, contains mostly discharge from storm drains and sewage plants.

As thousands of rivers and streams empty into our coasts, they can add to either the health or the decline of our living seas, depending on their own health. Here are some things you can do to assure that your local streams and rivers are healthy:

1. Learn about the watershed you live in, and become involved with your local watershed council. If there isn't one, work with a national organization to form one.

2. Help protect rivers and streams at the suburban fringe by promoting responsible development that includes natural buffer zones, such as parks and shade trees planted along riverbanks.

3. Help your community rediscover and revitalize its waterfront by getting involved in ecologically sound restoration projects and planning. Groups such as the Center for Watershed Protection can provide technical assistance.

4. Walk along a local stream or river. Learn about its history. Find out how the Clean Water Act of 1972 may have affected it. This information can help you enlist the support of others in restoration efforts.

5. Work with groups carrying out cleanup projects in your local streams and rivers. These may include high school and university classes and environmental, fishing, boating, or watershed groups. National organizations such as American Rivers can help connect you with these efforts.

6. Learn whether old irrigation and power dams in your watershed are still economical and environmentally useful. If not, work with watershed and fishing groups in your area and local, state, and federal agencies to start removing some of these obsolescent dams.

32. Live a Reasonable Distance from the Beach

Your commonsense precautions can keep your home from being destroyed and demonstrate how to live in harmony with the sea.

Until 1968 when the federal government got into the business of providing flood insurance to private landowners, few people built their homes on or right next to the shore. Those who did, either built beach shacks and small cottages they could afford to lose in a storm or were rich enough to risk building larger summer homes without insurance. Now, with federal flood insurance inspiring banks to provide mortgages in high-risk coastal zones, millions of people are living right by the beach, or even on the sand, "reserving front-row seats at the water's edge," as one magazine described it. This despite a report by the Federal Emergency Management Agency (FEMA) that erosion and rising sea levels from climate change will, over the next 50 years, destroy one out of four homes built within 500 feet of the sea.

Florida's terrible hurricane season of 2004 and the far more devastating Katrina disaster of 2005 exposed the risk. Building on barrier islands, on beaches, or on filled-in wetlands and salt marshes not only puts your home and family at risk but also contributes to the degradation of coastal ecosystems that normally act as storm barriers.

"It used to be that everyone built well back from the beach," says Robert Davis, who developed Seaside, Florida. When a hurricane struck the Florida panhandle in 1995, his planned community, built behind protective dunes and to standards above those in the hurricane code, survived intact, while neighboring beachfront communities were destroyed. Since then, other coastal developments, such as Watercolor, Florida, and Shorepine, Oregon, have followed the Seaside model of building in harmony with coastal dunes and natural storm barriers. Coastal living can be a great experience as long as you build and buy with great respect for the natural processes of the coast. Here's how to do that:

1. Obtain a geological and hydrological assessment of the area where you're thinking of buying.

2. Order copies of FEMA's flood hazard maps to see if the area you're looking at is at risk.

3. Consider homes that are not on the water but easily accessible to the beach by bike or walking trails.

4. Buy a home that is well above sea level or is behind barrier islands, which block storms that would otherwise devastate the mainland.

5. Encourage friends and relatives who are considering moving to the beach to move "close to the beach" instead.

6. Look to purchase existing housing stock rather than buying in new developments that contribute to coastal sprawl.

7. Learn about programs like the Coastal Barrier Resources Act (CBRA) that help protect high-risk natural areas from harmful development while adding value to adjacent communities.

33. Count the Fish; Then Do Some Light Housekeeping for Them

Dive for science, conservation, and adventure.

For centuries, scientists and naturalists have studied and counted terrestrial creatures and their habitats to understand the world better. But it was only in 1992 that Dr. Gary Davis, a scientist with the Channel Islands National Park in California, thought to establish the Great Annual Fish Count (GAFC) as a way to encourage sports divers to report their fish sightings. Based on the Audubon Society's annual Christmas Bird Count, the GAFC started modestly with 50 divers in the waters of the Channel's Anacapa Island. Today the fish count takes place every year throughout July in a wide variety of locations from Hawaii to Canada. Thousands of diver volunteers and their collected data are coordinated by the Reef Environmental Education Foundation (REEF), with support from the National Marine Sanctuary Program. The count raises public awareness about trends in fish populations, provides scientists and the public with new information, offers a useful nonextractive recreational diving activity, and improves fish-population assessment techniques.

Every year some of these same volunteer divers return to the sea either to join the International Coastal Cleanup that takes place every September (see action 27), or to take part in local efforts, such as the Avalon Harbor Underwater Cleanup on Catalina Island each February, which draws about 500 divers. More than 125,000 divers have participated in underwater cleanup efforts over the last decade. They use mesh bags to collect most trash and sometimes use lift bags to remove heavy items such as tires from deep water.

While underwater cleanups can save marine wildlife and improve the look of popular dive sites, they need to be done carefully in ways that don't damage ocean resources. So gear up, and follow these directions:

1. Attend a free fish-identification seminar and pre-dive meeting in your area to see whether you'd like to be part of the Great Annual Fish Count. Information on meetings is provided through REEF or at www.fishcount.org.

2. Learn the history of fish and marine wildlife populations in your area from marine biologists at your local university or research lab or from groups like the Marine Fish Conservation Network. Find out what factors have adversely affected them.

3. Join an organized underwater cleanup through your local dive shop, Project AWARE (see Resources), or other groups; make sure that the group knows how to dive safely, has experience, and plans its dives.

4. Wear protective gloves during your underwater cleanup.

5. Avoid damage to marine life. Collect only debris that does not have any growth on it. Do not disturb wildlife. Check container debris for possible residents (crabs, octopuses, and the like) before removing it. Use clippers, rather than a knife, to cut free entangled animals you many encounter.

6. Remove new fishing line (without growth on it) to reduce risk of entanglement by marine creatures. Cut the line using clippers or scissors. Take the end and coil it loosely around your hand or snugly around a bottle or other debris item. Swim along the line as you coil it. If you hit resistance don't tug—you could rip a sponge or tip a coral head. Investigate, and, if necessary, cut the line and begin the process over again.

34. Protect the Dunes So They'll Protect Us

Sand dunes protect the beach naturally, provided they aren't damaged or removed.

Coastal sand dunes are created and shaped by wind and tide. Sands deposited by rivers and offshore currents build them into physical barriers that protect the coastline and inland areas from saltwater intrusion and erosion while also absorbing wave energy in ways that keep the soft beach from eroding away. Dunes protect coastal populations from flooding during coastal storms and act as homes and shelters for a variety of plants, animals, nesting sea turtles, and shorebirds. Beaches, barrier islands, and coastal sand dunes are dynamic, changing natural systems. Like geology with the fast-forward button always on, they change with weather, tides, and storms.

As developers have built homes and high-rises on our country's beaches, they've knocked down many dunes and then tried to stabilize the newly exposed sand with seawalls and jetties. Unfortunately, these constructions actually increase erosion. Jetties steal sand from the nearshore current running parallel with the land. This builds up the beach on one side of the jetty and erodes beaches farther down the shore. Not wanting to see their beaches turn to rock cobble, neighboring property owners begin to build more and longer jetties. Geologists call this the "New Jerseyfication" of the shore. Seawalls also concentrate wave action, which then undermines the walls and eventually turns them into rubble.

Other human constructions impairing the health of dunes are dams and water diversion structures on coastal rivers, which reduce upland sand flow to the beach.

One response has been multimillion-dollar "beach restoration" projects carried out by the U.S. Army Corps of Engineers, whose contractors pump offshore sand onto degraded beaches. But this often alters the appearance and biological structure of the beach and can destroy offshore habitat for bottom fish, crabs, and other creatures. Instead, we need to work for the protection and restoration of existing sand dunes, along with wetlands and other natural storm barriers. Here's how you can help:

1. No matter how tempting it is to jump or slide down sand dunes, stick to established paths and elevated walkways to avoid damaging plants and animals that live in the dunes.

2. If you must drive on a beach, keep off the dunes, soft sand, and wetland areas.

3. Leave seaweed and driftwood where you find them. They provide food, habitat, and shelter for various beach animals.

4. Join local dune restoration programs run by groups like the Dunes Center in California. Their activities may include replacing non-native species with native plants, like American dune grass or beach bursage. Native plants help to stabilize the dunes and keep them in place.

35. Power Down around Whales, Manatees, and Other Marine Wildlife

Good boating behavior respects marine animals.

There are fewer than 300 northern right whales left in the world. They got their name from the fact that they tend to stay near the surface for long intervals and don't seem afraid of humans, so New England whalers called them the "right whale" to kill. More recently it's accidental but deadly strikes from large ships and entanglements in fishing gear that are the main threats to the survival of this species.

Closer to shore along the warm waters of the coast of Florida you'll find the last 3,000 manatees, giant, gentle herbivores (plant eaters) that can live for up to 60 years and weigh up to 1,200 pounds each. Manatees are large, gray aquatic mammals with thick bodies that taper to flat paddle tails. They have wrinkled faces and whiskered snouts. Their closest relatives are the elephant and the hyrax, a small gopherlike mammal. They're also related to the Steller's sea cow, which was hunted to extinction in 1768. Among the range of threats that manatees face today, one of the biggest is being crushed or slashed to death by the hulls and propellers of fast-moving powerboats in the warm shallow waters these creatures favor. They are especially vulnerable in the winter months when, like so many rotund tourists, they congregate in Florida.

Boating behavior affects many other animals, including sea turtles when they're near the surface, breathing or mating, and bird colonies that abandon their nesting sites if startled by loud noises from personal watercraft or fast-moving powerboats. Following basic rules of law and common sense can often avert a wildlife tragedy, as well as a boating accident:

1. Obey posted speed zone signs and no-wake signs, and keep away from posted manatee sanctuaries.

2. Wear polarized sunglasses to help eliminate glare and allow you to see below the water's surface when you operate a boat.

3. Stay in deep-water channels when boating. Avoid seagrass beds and shallow areas where manatees and green sea turtles might be feeding.

4. Chart the right course. Do your homework to know the waterways and channels you're using. Not only will you help prevent damage to animals and their habitats, but you'll also keep your boat from grounding.

5. If you like high-speed water sports such as water-skiing or racing personal watercraft, choose appropriate areas, like lakes or deep offshore waters.

6. Supervise teenagers if you allow them to drive high-speed vessels.

7. Keep at least 50 feet away when observing marine mammals such as manatees and dolphins. Use binoculars, a scope, or a zoom lens for a closer look. If you want to linger, cut your engine—but don't let your boat drift over the animal. Coming too close can stress the animals. If they're curious, they'll approach you.

8. If you observe anyone harassing, injuring, or endangering wildlife, report the lawbreaker to local authorities.

36. Join a Marine Mammal Rescue Center

Be the first responder for a marine animal in distress.

Not long ago I helped return two five-foot nurse sharks that had been raised in captivity to the clear tropical waters of the Florida Keys. While shark-wrangling may sound kind of macho, the fact is that among the other rescuers were several children, one of whom had to be admonished by her mom to "stop hugging the shark and pass her along." The restoration crew was coordinated by a former Navy dolphin trainer working with the local Marine Mammal Conservancy, one of dozens of groups, now found in every coastal state and territory, that respond to stranded wildlife.

These groups rescue, restore to health, and return to the wild aquatic animals that have been injured, orphaned, or stranded for various reasons. Many of the animals' injuries are linked to human activities like pollution, entangling fishing gear, and active military sonar or other noise disturbances.

Given permits by the government to treat and release seals, sea lions, dolphins, whales, and sea turtles, rescue centers are most often nonprofit operations in need of volunteer support. For example, the Marine Mammal Center headquartered in northern California relies on a network of more than 800 volunteers, who undergo the center's orientation and training. One of the most popular positions is in animal care, where volunteers help to feed, weigh, chart, and monitor animals, clean their pens and pools, and otherwise support their recovery. Other volunteers work as drivers or members of a rescue team, which checks out stranding reports and does rescues when called on. Rescue work requires extensive training. Education, research, communications, event planning, and fundraising are other areas in which volunteers can be active. Student intern positions are available at many of the stranding networks and centers. Here are a few additional tips:

1. Don't expect that you'll be able to befriend a wild creature at the center. Most rehabilitation efforts try to minimize human contact and association with food; animals that have become habituated to people can run into problems when they're returned to the wild.

2. Promptly report stranded or distressed marine animals to trained responders if you're not fully trained yourself. Don't try to help stranded animals on your own. Some animals, such as young seals, may appear to be orphaned but are actually under the watchful eye of a nearby parent. An animal that is sick or injured is also more likely to bite.

3. Take your volunteer spirit with you to the water. Educate your fellow beachgoers. If you notice people unwittingly behaving in a way that disturbs the wildlife, approach them in a friendly, respectful, and discrete way, and inform them of appropriate guidelines; if they seem to be intentionally hurting animals, call the local authorities.

4. Study why marine animals are becoming sick or stranded and which human activities may be at fault; for example, certain types of fishing gear are likely to entangle marine life. Become active in working to reduce the causes of the problem.

37. Work to Create Wilderness Parks under the Sea

Help to fully protect our last great frontier
wilderness and wildlife range.

Marine sanctuaries offer tremendous recreational opportunities, but they function like national forests, where logging and other industrial activities still take place, rather than like national parks, where wilderness is fully protected. In recent years, there have been growing calls to fully protect at least some of our unique marine wilderness areas as "national parks in the sea." These include spectacular coral reefs, kelp forests, and submarine mountains, and the sea life that inhabits them.

Beginning in the 1990s, marine scientists suggested that as much as 20 percent of the ocean needed to be set aside as no-take zones (sometimes called marine protected areas) if we hope to maintain the diversity of life that exists on our blue-ocean planet. As wilderness parks, these no-take zones would exclude fishing, harvesting of sand and kelp, drilling for oil and gas, and other consumptive uses of the sea.

Presently less than 0.1 percent of the world's oceans are protected as wilderness areas. Countries such as Australia, New Zealand, Columbia, Mexico, and Mozambique are far ahead of the United States in the percentage of their waters that they protect.

I've gone diving, snorkeling, and boating in marine wilderness parks off Florida, California, Belize, and elsewhere and have noticed the greater variety and abundance of fish and wildlife. Scientific studies confirm that these ecological reserves increase the number, size, and diversity of fish, shellfish, and other animals. They also document a "spillover effect": fish catches increase outside the parks. This is why some commercial fishermen support marine wilderness parks. Still, no-take zones remain controversial with other fishing groups, which object to the parks.

There are good reasons to support reserves aside from the increase in fish populations outside their boundaries. After all, Yellowstone wasn't founded so that elk hunting outside the park might be improved. It was founded to protect a unique wilderness and allow all Americans to experience it. Places such as the Northwest Hawaii Ecosystem Reserve, parts of the Gulf of Maine, deep waters off Alaska, and the Dry Tortugas off Florida hold the promise of becoming the new Yellowstones of the 21st century. These ocean wilderness parks in the making are places where we can experience our last great physical frontier in its natural state while also protecting it for future generations. Here's how you can help:

1. Contact your state marine or fish and wildlife agency to find out how much, if any, of your state coastal water is fully protected. California has passed a law—the Marine Life Protection Act—to establish a network of well-defined no-take zones along its 1,100 miles of coast.

2. If you live near a marine sanctuary or coastal national park or seashore, find out if its management plans include fully protected areas. If not, ask why not.

3. Talk to scientists, fishermen and women, divers, your neighbors, and other interested parties to begin a public dialogue about marine wilderness parks.

4. Contact and join environmental groups that are working to establish marine parks: the Ocean Conservancy, World Wildlife Fund, Conservation International, Environmental Defense, Shifting Baselines, and others (see Resources).

5. Evaluate the pro and con arguments, and get involved in the marine wilderness preservation battle while there are still wild seas to protect.

38. Don't Feed the Sharks (or Let Them Feed on You)

Feeding marine wildlife puts both animals
and people in danger.

I once went on a diving trip to Australia's Great Barrier Reef, where I watched the dive boat crew feeding giant potato cod (400-pound groupers) from a bucket. One big bruiser almost knocked me over trying to get to the "feeding station." Tragically, one of the boat's crew was later found dead on the bottom. He'd been free diving and, they suspected, had been knocked unconscious by a large fish that had come to associate divers with food.

In the 1950s and 1960s many people visiting Yellowstone Park used to feed grizzly bears alongside the roads. When I was a small child in New Hampshire people liked to go to the local dump to watch the black bears feed on garbage. Since then, people have realized that letting bears and other potentially dangerous wildlife associate people with food invites disaster, usually for the wild animals, which become "nuisances" and have to be killed, but sometimes for people as well.

Our explorations of the ocean are much more recent than those of the land. To date we've failed to apply some of the lessons we learned from interacting with terrestrial wildlife. I've been on dive trips where the guides harassed octopuses to make them squirt their ink, hand-fed moray eels and barracuda, and lured sharks with dead fish.

In fact, shark dives where sharks are lured to divers with food have become a popular but dangerous form of recreational entertainment. A proposed white shark cage dive operation was banned in California's Monterey Bay National Marine Sanctuary when the businessman promoting it announced he would attract these top predators by spreading fish blood on the water within a mile of where surfers and kayakers were enjoying themselves.

Now Florida, Hawaii, and other states have banned shark feeding, and people are learning that a real marine wildlife experience is one that doesn't change the habits and behaviors of the creatures they're swimming with or observing. Here are some ways to protect marine wildlife from associating people with food:

1. Don't feed marine animals from boats or while in the water.

2. If you're catching fish, clean them in different locales, so you don't attract predators to the same spot every time.

3. When you go on a chartered boat dive, chose a reputable dive operation that doesn't use food lures to attract marine wildlife.

4. Don't grab, pull the tails of, or otherwise harass sharks. Even benign species such as nurse sharks have been known to bite people when harassed.

5. Be respectful of sharks, sea lions, barracuda, and other top marine predators. If they begin to exhibit aggressive behavior leave the water for a time.

39. Don't Exploit Sea Creatures for Vanity's Sake

Heed Jacques Cousteau's warning:
"The sea is not a bargain basement."

From coral jewelry to coral calcium, nautilus shells to ground seahorse, turtle oil to shark liver oil, a range of decorative items and supposed health products from the sea are creating profitable markets while depleting the ocean's natural bounty.

"Semiprecious" black corals are heavily exploited for jewelry even though they're protected by many nations. To collect deep-ocean pink corals, which take hundreds of years to grow, chains are dragged across the sea bottom, and the broken pieces of coral that become caught in their links are then used for making jewelry. Left behind is the rubble of unique once-living ecosystems.

More than 100 million slow-breeding sharks are killed every year for their fins, which are used in a tasteless but expensive (and thus high status) soup popular in China. Shark body parts are also used in so-called health products popular in the West, including shark liver oil and shark cartilage. The unsubstantiated benefits claimed for these products in fighting cancer led to a government warning and court injunction against one manufacturer.

By protecting marine ecosystems we're also protecting a biological treasure trove of potential cures and treatments for human ills that can be harvested without abusing the sea. Two widely used drugs—Acyclovir, which treats herpes, and AZT, which fights the HIV-AIDS virus—are derived from compounds first identified in marine sponges. Many other potentially useful drugs are now being developed from marine organisms, including cancer-fighting compounds from soft corals, anti-inflammation chemicals from sea feathers, virus-killing proteins from sea grass molds, and painkillers from cone snails. Scientists involved in prospecting for these promising new biological treatments are also working to synthesize them in the lab, in order to protect rather than deplete the marine sources and habitats that produce them. Here's how you can help protect the seas' natural resources, which could someday save your life or that of a loved one:

1. Don't purchase coral jewelry or other products made from this threatened marine creature (corals are living colonial animals, not decorative rocks).

2. Don't purchase dietary supplements made from endangered wildlife like coral calcium, shark cartilage, turtle oil, or shark liver oil. Useful nutrients such as vitamin A, found in shark liver oil, can also be acquired by eating dark green vegetables.

3. Don't purchase dried sea horses for decoration or folk medicines that falsely claim to cure asthma, impotence, and the like. Sea horses are an endangered species.

4. Become an eco-savvy shopper and beachcomber. Educate
   yourself about which marine products are at risk and which
   are not (rare shells as opposed to sea glass, for example)
   and collect or purchase accordingly.

40. Keep Oil off Our Shore

We can develop ocean-friendly sources of
energy on and off the water.

In the 1980s, President Ronald Reagan proposed opening up
a billion acres of offshore United States waters to oil and gas
drilling. Broad-based popular opposition to this plan led to the
establishment of three major national marine sanctuaries off
California, Florida, and Massachusetts where oil drilling is forbidden by law. In addition, Congress passed a moratorium on
any new oil drilling. In effect for more than 25 years, the moratorium prevents drilling off the East and West coasts and parts
of the Gulf of Mexico. But with rising oil and gas prices and the
disastrous hurricanes in the Gulf in 2005, the energy industry
and Washington politicians are pushing to reopen offshore
waters. Their first step came with the 2005 Energy Act, which
authorized an oil and gas survey of all previously protected
waters.

At the same time, a new anti-oil coalition is emerging. It
brings together conservationists concerned about the threat of
fossil-fuel-driven global warming and political conservatives

worried about the nation's growing dependence on Middle-Eastern oil suppliers, some with links to terrorism. These activists have begun to advocate for new noncarbon energy alternatives.

The question for each of us is: What type of energy future are we going to have—one that protects our natural resources, or one that threatens to destroy them? Some advocate a nonpolluting ocean energy plan. There are plans, for example, to install big power-generating tidal turbines at the entrance to San Francisco Bay. Another proposal is to produce ocean thermal energy; this was first tested on the Big Island of Hawaii. Why not learn to harness the clean energy at our disposal, rather than continuing down a path of dependence on nonsustainable, environmentally harmful energy sources?

Energy policy decisions that will affect our oceans, climate, weather, water, and food supply are too important to leave to politicians and the energy industry alone. That's why we each have to make some decisions. Here's how to start:

1. Learn about the costs of energy. Talk to your gas station manager and power company officials. Find out what kind of power your local plant uses—coal? Diesel? Natural gas? Where is your local gasoline refinery located? What plans for new energy facilities have local officials agreed to, and how do those fit into a larger clean energy vision?

2. Read up on new energy technologies in books like *The Hydrogen Economy* and *The End of Oil,* and talk to neighbors, friends, scientists, and economists about the possibilities of changing from an oil-based economy.

3. If your power company offers "green energy" options, switch to one of them.

4. Work with ocean conservation groups and your state and congressional delegations to protect coastal waters from

high-risk oil and gas drilling or from liquefied natural gas platforms if they pose environmental or security risks. Groups such as the OCS (Outer Continental Shelf) Coalition can help you make these contacts.

5. Learn about solar, wind, and other alternative energy systems, and see if they make sense for your home. Find out if your local power company will buy surplus energy from you if you go "off the grid" this way.

section

5

Learn and Share

41. Visit an Aquarium

Learn about the amazing diversity of life
in the sea and how to protect it.

People have kept fish in enclosures for more than 2,500 years, mostly for food. The first aquarium designed for public display opened in Regents Park, London, in 1853. Three years later, P. T. Barnum opened an aquarium of "curious creatures" from the sea in New York City. Today some 40 million Americans a year visit dozens of public aquariums. The larger and better known among them include the Monterey Bay Aquarium, the Aquarium of the Pacific in Long Beach, California, the New England Aquarium in Boston, the National Aquarium in Baltimore, and the Shedd Aquarium in Chicago.

In recent years, as the crisis in our seas has deepened, many nonprofit aquariums have moved from acting as "fish zoos" to becoming major advocates and educators for ocean conservation. "We want to reach people at the point of inspiration," says Glenn Page, Director of Conservation for the

National Aquarium in Baltimore. "The Blue Vision we're looking at involves outreach and engagement with the public so we don't become displays of what habitat used to look like." That aquarium is involved in local restoration efforts in Baltimore Harbor and the larger Chesapeake Bay, working with volunteers to clean shorelines and plant marsh grass in order to reduce erosion and restore wildlife habitat. The staff also does work in other areas, including Ocean City, Maryland, and the Bahamas.

The New England Aquarium was the first to have a conservation department. Today it's working to study and protect endangered northern right whales off of Boston, and producing educational films on issues such as the impact of climate change on the ocean environment. Many aquariums have ocean exploration and conservation lecture series. Still others provide educational opportunities for schoolchildren. The small but impressive Dauphin Island Sea Lab Estuarium in Alabama hosts thousands of students a year through its Discovery Hall Programs.

A few aquariums have been pivotal in changing public attitudes about certain sea creatures, such as sharks. One turning point involved a great white shark caught in a fisherman's net off California in August 1980. The young 300-pound female, named Sandy (after the fisherman's ex-wife), was trucked to the Steinhart Aquarium in San Francisco where she was kept in a large tank for 72 hours. While there, Sandy was visited by the mayor, the national media, and thousands of tourists. CBS anchor Walter Cronkite dubbed her "the darling of San Francisco." Unable to get the shark to feed, the aquarium staff decided to release her back into the wild, which they did from a charter boat. Sandy inspired a sea change: the public recognized the importance of having top predators like great white sharks in the sea.

Today, many aquariums are working to help consumers make informed choices about the seafood they consume. The Monterey Bay Aquarium's Seafood Watch program, for example, has developed a Seafood Pocket Guide to help visitors chose the most sustainable seafood when shopping or going to restaurants (see action 13).

Aquariums also work to preserve animals and their habitats through research and spawning programs. By breeding and nurturing juveniles in their tanks they hope to restore depleted populations of sea horses, sharks, groupers, and other threatened species. They are active in marine mammal rescue programs as well. You, too, can be a part of this exciting work by doing the following:

1. Join your local aquarium.

2. Get involved in an aquarium volunteer program.

3. If you're a student, investigate the internship programs that many aquariums offer.

4. Learn which conservation and community development efforts your local aquarium sponsors.

5. Learn about the best standards and practices for aquariums from the American Zoo and Aquarium Association, and make sure your community aquarium is meeting these standards.

6. Organize a visit to the nearest aquarium for your workplace, school, community group, or place of worship, and volunteer as a group for the aquarium's conservation-related activities.

42. Support Marine Education in Our Schools

Education is the key to understanding the seas around us.

When I was nine years old, Mrs. Olson, my fourth-grade teacher, brought a couple of six-foot sawfish bills into class. These were the sharp, flat, serrated snouts of large, dangerous looking sea creatures closely related to both sharks and rays. Hawaiian warriors once used sawfish bills as broad swords, deadly weapons of war. Mrs. Olson's father, a Long Island sea captain who had captured the giant fish, had given her the bills. Today sawfish are an endangered species as a result of both targeted fishing and what's called bycatch—the fish are caught when their bills become entangled in the nets of fishing boats chasing after other species.

Four decades after Mrs. Olson wowed our class, I still remember this bit of show-and-tell as a turning point in my love for and fascination with the sea. There is a popular environmental saying that "We will conserve only what we love; we will love only what we understand; and we will understand only what we have been taught." Education is a key to understanding the sea around us. Today more than half the United States population lives in coastal zones, yet few elementary, middle, or high schools incorporate marine education into their core curriculums, even in Florida, California, Alaska, and Hawaii. A few magnet schools and educational efforts now underway have begun moving in the right direction. You can help turn the tide with the following actions:

1. Contact the National Marine Educators Association and learn what resources it (and its regional affiliates) have for your school and teachers. Share this information at your local school board meeting and with your children's teachers.

2. Learn more about ongoing marine projects at the Mast Academy in Miami, the Harbor School in New York City, and similar programs in California and elsewhere that might make sense for your school district.

3. Find opportunities for your school to participate in local beach cleanups and other coastal and ocean conservation events. You can learn about them through groups such as the Ocean Conservancy (see Resources), which sponsors an International Coastal Cleanup Day in September.

4. Use Internet sites such as The Jason Project, EarthEcho International, Khaled bin Sultan Living Oceans Foundation, and the National Oceanographic and Atmospheric Administration's Ocean Explorer site (see Resources) to link classrooms to real-time ocean expeditions, explorations, and learning opportunities.

5. Organize a school trip to your local aquarium or marine science center.

6. Have your school invite someone from the coast guard or other marine agency to speak with the students about what he or she does.

43. Speak for the Seas at Local Public Hearings

Active citizenship can help restore our oceans and coasts.

More than half the United States population lives near the seacoast, where development is booming (some say sprawling). In California, 80 percent of the residents now live in coastal counties. Of the nation's 20 fastest growing counties, 17 are coastal; of the 20 largest cities, 14 are coastal. Cities and townships are where most decisions about growth and planning are made. That's why they are such vital government links in ensuring that your coast and ocean are protected. Don't think you have to travel to Washington or your state capitol; you can affect government decisions by attending local public hearings.

Local zoning boards set building and land use standards that can determine the impact of construction and development on coastal waters and the watersheds that feed into them. A zoning board meeting is a good place to speak out in favor of protecting local wetlands and recreational beaches and of setting high standards of environmental protection for your neighborhood. Departments of sanitation, public works departments, and sewage districts maintain services vital to healthy oceans, including sewage plants, sewage pipes, and storm drains. At these agencies you can advocate for the most advanced treatment to reduce pollution and make sure that the existing infrastructure isn't being outstripped by growth. Public health departments track the safety of swimming water and locally caught fish but don't always provide enough public warning or take precautionary measures unless they feel pressure from the public. Water boards allocate water resource use. Developer and agricultural interests often attend meetings of or serve on these boards, but too few people work with them to promote the benefits of maintaining free-flowing water for fish, wildlife, and coastal habitat. Park departments establish, maintain, and protect recreational beaches and coastal parks. Your good citizenship and participation at the local level can help keep our oceans and coasts healthy and abundant or restore them to that state.

1. Working with the local media and public records (zoning board applications, requests for variances on building permits), become aware of projects or activities that may threaten your waters. Attend your local zoning board or planning board meetings, and voice your concerns.

2. Maintain a community watch of concerned citizens. Construction near wetlands and waterways requires permits, and erosion-control measures are mandatory. Your local planning department can verify if these permits have been issued. If not, report violations you observe to local authorities or permitting agencies such as the federal Army Corps of Engineers and Environmental Protection Agency.

3. Arrange for a tour of your local water-treatment and waste-water (sewage) plants with friends, neighbors, or a community

group. Learn if your community has advanced wastewater treatment and uses environmentally friendly technologies. If not, campaign for needed change.

4. If you feel that local officials aren't making the connection between healthy waters and vibrant coastal communities and economies, consider running, or supporting a friend to run, for local office.

44. Learn Your Local Maritime History

Knowing what our oceans have been means knowing what they can be.

The catastrophe of Hurricane Katrina in 2005 was made worse by the fact that many people ignored the lessons of the past (about cycles of hurricane activity, the importance of wetlands, how to build safely by the shore, and how to prepare for the worst). Only by knowing where we come from can we hope to understand where we are and where we might be headed. New York City offers another example: there, 80 percent of the land is on islands separated from the mainland. Henry Hudson first anchored at Manhattan because of its well-protected harbor, rich in fish and oysters. Shipbuilding was a mainstay of colonial America, and New York soon became known as a great port. But by the 20th century New York harbor and the Hudson River feeding into it were polluted, many people thought beyond redemption. Only when some Hudson River fishermen began researching 19th-century water law, and folksinger Pete Seeger launched a 106-foot replica of a historic Hudson River sloop called The Clearwater, were antipollution forces able to turn the bleak picture around, bringing New York's waters back to their historic glory.

On both East and West coasts, and along the Gulf, we are rediscovering our maritime roots: from restoring historic water-fronts in New Bedford, Massachusetts, New York City, Baltimore, and Long Beach, California, to establishing maritime centers, surfing museums, and harbor schools. People are reconnecting with the past and using it as a basis for planning a healthier blue future.

The Chesapeake Bay Foundation uses a historic rating system in its conservation work. It rates the bay's ecological health as 100 when European explorers first settled it. Today the health rating is 25, but the foundation believes that, through restoration and best environmental practices, it could be restored to 75.

Understandably people tend to look only at changes that have taken place in their lifetimes, dismissing the tales of old-timers as products of nostalgia. That's how our understanding of what's "natural" keeps shifting. But new historical and scientific techniques show our natural and cultural seafaring heritage to be far richer than we've previously believed. Instead of 25,000 humpback whales in the Atlantic before modern whaling, as the International Whaling Commission once believed, DNA testing suggests there may have been 500,000. We're also coming to realize that, along with land surveyors like Lewis and Clark, some of America's most intrepid explorers were sailors such as Nathaniel Palmer, a Connecticut seal hunter. In 1820 at the age of 21, Palmer, sailing a small boat, was the first person to discover the continent of Antarctica. In 1960 Don Walsh, riding in the bathysphere *Trieste,* became one of only two humans ever to touch down on the deepest spot on earth, the Marianas Trench, seven miles below the surface of the Pacific. They and countless others represent our maritime heritage, the blue in our red, white, and blue.

Learning more about your local maritime and marine history is a great way to find the kind of inspiration you may need to help save the ocean.

1. Visit your nearest maritime museum.

2. Find out about historical research or archives on local ocean conditions and events at your community college or university, and see if these centers of information need volunteer help.

3. Involve your local high school or community group in a maritime history project.

4. Interview retired fishermen and women, dockworkers, lifeguards, shipyard operators, merchant marine veterans, scientists, and others along the shore. Record their stories of the sea.

5. Help organize a local maritime festival commemoration or historic reenactment.

45. Talk to Your Cousin in Kansas about the Weather

Become an educator on how the oceans affect us all.

Not long ago I gave a speech about the oceans at a college in Minnesota. It was February and there was snow on the ground. "So why should you be interested in the oceans?" I asked rhetorically. "Well, let's take a deep breath and ponder that . . . . Oh, wait, that's right—most of the oxygen we're breathing comes from the sea." While the rainforests have been called the lungs of the planet, tiny plankton in the world's oceans actually absorb most of the carbon dioxide in the atmosphere and return 70 percent of the oxygen we need to live. The oceans are also drivers of weather and climate. Meteorologists look to the sky to predict tomorrow's weather, but for long-range forecasting they're increasingly looking to the sea.

Scientists creating three-dimensional "weather maps" of the ocean track cold-water upwellings, cold spots, and warm spots. Phenomena such as El Niños, which are linked to a warming in the eastern and central Pacific, have global effects, leading to major droughts, forest fires, crop failures, and coral bleaching. A periodic one-degree warming in the north Atlantic creates 25- to 30-year cycles of lesser and greater hurricane intensity, which contributed to the ferocity of the 2004 and 2005 hurricane seasons.

The oceans also act as a sponge, or what scientists call a sink, for excess carbon dioxide generated by the burning of fossil fuels. This has slowed the rate of global warming in the atmosphere. Unfortunately, it has also led to warming seas, rising sea levels, stronger El Niños, changes in oceanic productivity, and acidification of ocean waters.

The oceans are also absorbing far more nitrogen and phosphorus than at any time in recent planetary history because of urban and agricultural runoff. According to major scientific studies, the planet's nitrogen cycle has doubled in the last 50 years with the use of petrochemical fertilizers and fuels. The nitrogen increase has generated algae blooms and dead zones in coastal oceans throughout the world. Coal-fired power plants and industrial factories also deposit mercury and other toxins in our ocean waters, and these elements then work their way back up the food web to us.

These examples demonstrate not only how the oceans are intricately linked to all other environmental processes but also how our actions can affect planetary-scale processes, so that we end up having an impact on not just our local waters but even our weather and the air we breath.

Because these ocean processes affect people throughout the world, we must talk about what all of us can do wherever we live, not only in coastal communities. Here's how to learn more and then educate others who don't live on a coast:

1. Share your favorite ocean books, television programs, and DVDs with friends and relatives who live inland.

2. Learn how nitrogen and phosphorus runoff from farms in the Midwest adversely affects the Gulf of Mexico and other

coastal areas and what some farmers are doing to reduce runoff.

3. Work to promote family farming and local farmers' markets. Small, diverse farms require fewer chemical inputs and generate less waste than industrial farming.

4. Talk to friends around the country about how coal-fired power plants release mercury into the atmosphere that ends up in the tuna and other seafood we consume.

5. Encourage your inland friends and relatives to join ocean conservation efforts that you support, and in exchange offer to work on issues that are closest to their hearts.

46. Learn How to Navigate and Read the Tides

HANG IN THERE. THE TIDE WILL BE BACK AGAIN IN... UHHH... FOUR HOURS AND TWENTY-THREE MINUTES.

Understanding the movement of the ocean keeps us safe and connected.

Tides reflect the regular rising and falling of the ocean's surface caused by forces of gravity beyond the earth, mainly the gravitational field of the moon but secondarily that of the sun. Tides change not only in depth but also in the direction of their currents. There are normally two high tides and two low tides each day. Tidal changes along various coastlines, bays, and rivers can range from a few inches to the spectacular tides in the Bay of Fundy, Canada, where water levels can change 50 feet. Tidal charts that keep track of these changes are essential reading for boat captains, surfers (tides affect wave form and create rips), clammers, beachcombers, and coastal residents.

Navigating the waters between the tides has been one of the great challenges for ocean explorers, from Polynesian seafarers, who colonized the Pacific using celestial knowledge and a keen sea sense, to Europe's mercantile fleets, which took centuries to position longitude in relation to latitude (with the invention of the chromatograph) so that they could accurately chart their courses. Today, navigational charts are going digital, while hand-held satellite global positioning system (GPS) devices can tell you within feet what your position is anywhere on the surface of the planet. (One time, when I was shipwrecked in Mexico, my companion noted that our GPS let us know "exactly where we're lost.")

Despite our impressive technologies we've still accurately mapped only about 10 percent of our oceans' topography at the resolution we use to map land, whether on earth, the moon, or Mars.

You can learn basic navigation and sailing skills early in life through Sea Scouting and other at-sea training programs. Knowing where you're going and when the tides will turn can give you a powerful edge in living well with and on the seas.

1. Learn to read tidal charts (available with instructions at most marine supply stores and listed in many local newspapers). This skill can help you select the best times for tidepooling, surfing, and hiking along exposed beach trails. It puts you in touch with the rhythms of the sea.

2. Take a coastal navigation course. Like a basic boating safety course, it can prove both fascinating and, on occasion, a lifesaver.

3. Study your navigation charts thoroughly, and compare them with visual cues on the land (buildings, mountains, cliffs) and buoys in the water. Know how to read scale (indicating latitude), depths, features, elevation notes, source classification, and symbol references on your charts before you set sail.

4. Learn to read buoys and other aids to navigation, so that you find the right channels and places to get past barriers

and through offshore traffic. You'll avoid running aground, damaging the habitat, and hurting your pride (or worse).

5. If you aspire to be a blue-water sailor, take advanced navigation training with paper, sextant, and compass. The challenge is worth the effort, especially if your electronic equipment fails you.

6. Equip your boat with good tools such as depth-finding sonar, a GPS, a marine radio, a compass, and an Emergency Position Indicating Radio Beacon (EPIRB).

47. Immerse Yourself in Blue Media

The ocean inspires works of music, art, literature, film, and television that send ripples through our souls.

From sea chanteys to hula to the works of Jimmy Buffett, Brian Wilson, and surfer/songwriter Jack Johnson, the ocean has offered its syncopated appeal to American musicians of every age, race, and disposition.

In painting Winslow Homer was perhaps America's greatest marine artist, although today the ocean inspires a range of stylists from Wyland, whose life-size whale murals cover warehouses and skyscrapers, to Alaskan illustrator Ray Troll, with his ironic icons of *Planet Ocean,* to cartoonist Jim Toomey, creator of the *Sherman's Lagoon* comic strip, whose works grace these pages.

Richard Henry Dana's *Two Years before the Mast* and Herman Melville's *Moby Dick* gave 19th-century Americans a realistic sense of the sea, as did the works of Jack London, John

Steinbeck, Rachel Carson, and others in the 20th century. Contemporary ocean writers include Peter Benchley, John McPhee, Sabastian Junger, Carl Safina, Susan Casey, and way too many others for me to list or even have time to read in depth.

Underwater and ocean photography has made amazing strides in the capable hands of people such as David Doubilet, Flip Nicklin, Victoria McCormick, Walcott Henry, and Wayne Levin, producer of surprising black-and-white images of Hawaii.

The books, films, and television specials of ocean explorer Jacques Cousteau made whole generations aware of "the silent world" of the sea. More fictional fare, including *Sea Hunt* and *Flipper* (the dolphin Lassie), added to audience awareness of the seas. From *Gidget to Bay Watch, Endless Summer* to *Riding Giants, Twenty Thousand Leagues under the Sea* (the movie) to *Finding Nemo* (the animated movie), the ocean has been a popular theme for popular culture.

Today new underwater film techniques and lighting, dive technology, and communications are bringing the seas to us in new and engaging ways. These range from "critter cams" mounted on seals, sharks, and whales that broadcast online and on television, to giant 3-D IMAX films about the ocean, some made by leading Hollywood directors like James Cameron.

Media can bring millions of people to greater awareness of our ocean planet and the challenges it faces. Here are some media-savvy things you can do:

1. Sit down with family and friends to recall every ocean-based movie that has affected or moved you. *Jaws? The Abyss? To Have and Have Not? Master and Commander? Das Boot? Le Grand Bleu (The Big Blue)? The Little Mermaid? Whale Rider?* Check your video/DVD store or service, and agree on one to rent and view together.

2. Watch a surf movie if you haven't already. They can be as exhilarating and hypnotic as the sea. Among the classics consider *Endless Summer, Big Wednesday, Step into Liquid, Riding Giants, Blue Crush, Five Summer Stories,* and early releases by director Bruce Brown such as *Slippery When Wet* (1958).

3. Introduce a new generation to Jacques Cousteau's many film and television works that are still available (on DVD) and books.

4. Enjoy marine-themed music, whether played by Dick Dale, the Beach Boys, or Sheryl Crow. Also try listening to some you may not be familiar with, such as Hawaiian or Cajun music or Canadian maritime songs performed by Great Big Sea.

5. Read great fiction and nonfiction about the sea. If you're part of a book club, suggest a selection that relates to an ocean theme.

6. Attend an ocean celebration such as the Mermaid Parade, "the nation's largest art parade," in Coney Island, New York, or the San Clemente Ocean Festival "celebrating surf, sun, and family fun," in Southern California.

7. Create your own statement about our blue planet through graphic art, design, photography, music, or any other medium of expression that suits you.

48. Go on a Live or Virtual Ocean Expedition

You can be part of ocean science exploration that is helping to preserve our last frontier.

According to ocean explorer and scientist Sylvia Earle, we've learned more about the oceans in the past 25 years than in the previous 25,000. That's because of advances in research ships and scientific platforms, diving technologies, climb-aboard submersibles, remote and autonomous underwater vehicles, side-scan sonar, multibeam and airborne surveillance systems, miniaturized tracking devices, and space-based remote sensing systems. These technologies have allowed us to expand our knowledge of the seas and our impacts on them.

Scientific projects now underway include creation of a Global Ocean Observation System and an active and ongoing Census of Marine Life that will greatly inform efforts to save marine wildlife. As bold as these projects are, students and everyday citizens can observe and actually participate in them. Opportunities range from helping count fish off the Big Island of Hawaii as a student intern to testing water quality as a high school student in New York. You can join an expedition aboard a Russian icebreaker or deep-diving submersible in the Arctic, or visit Antarctica, and the deepest parts of the ocean as a tourist (for a huge sum of money). In between these extremes, well-established nonprofit groups such as Earthwatch Institute match volunteers, who pay a fee to participate, with field scientists and projects. Numerous marine conservation science projects, ranging from Australia's Great Barrier Reef to the Florida Keys, seek volunteers. Here's how you can become involved:

1. Encourage your school, or your child's school, to participate in ocean projects such as the "Learning Ocean Science through Ocean Exploration" curriculum for grades 6 to 12 run by the National Oceanic and Atmospheric Administration Ocean Explorer program.

2. Call your local marine science center or university-based marine program to find out what public programs, lectures, links, and internships they offer.

3. Investigate marine expeditions and sea classes run by Earthwatch, Reef Check Foundation, Sea Education Association (SEA), and other reputable nonprofit organizations that seek interns, students, volunteers, or paying participants.

4. Find the many real-time and near-real-time Web links from the Aquarius Lab to the Gulf of Maine that offer online at-sea and underwater exploration and viewing.

5. Invite an ocean scientist or explorer to talk to your school, civic group, or other social gathering.

49. Vote for Those Who Protect the Coast

Let your elected representatives know that you evaluate them and vote on how they treat the coast and ocean.

"California is a place where you can still get elected running against offshore oil and for protection of the coast," argues Representative Sam Farr, a Democrat from California's central coast. Republican Representative Jim Saxton of New Jersey claims the same for his state. "In 1987 and 1988 we had a disaster with our coastal economy because of beach closures, algae blooms, medical waste, and dolphins washing up dead on our beaches," he explains. "We made a lot of needed changes in response to that."

"I believe all the ocean issues will get dealt with when people demand we take action," adds Curt Weldon, a Republican representative from Pennsylvania. "My district's not on the ocean but my people go to the ocean to enjoy themselves . . . . Protecting the oceans is too important to be seen as a partisan issue. No party can own it."

The House Oceans Caucus, of which these three representatives are members, is one of the few bipartisan groups still
functioning on Capitol Hill. The caucus is working hard to
enact and implement policy recommendations from two major
United States ocean commissions. Several states, including
California, Massachusetts, and Rhode Island, have joined the
effort. Unfortunately, without strong pressure from voters, too
few politicians have made protecting, exploring, and restoring
our public seas priority issues.

Retired Admiral Jim Watkins, chair of the U.S.
Commission on Ocean Policy, has warned that we may have
only five to ten years left to save our oceans before it's too late.
Still the White House and Congress take a wait-and-see attitude.
They could be waiting to see whether those who elected them
demand that they take action. It's up to each of us to meet that
challenge.

1. Learn who your local and national elected representatives
   are and where they stand on key ocean protection measures.

2. Write or call your elected officials to tell them that your support will depend on their taking strong conservation
   positions on these issues.

3. Encourage your local member of Congress to join the bipartisan House Oceans Caucus and support its comprehensive
   ocean-protection agenda.

4. Work with local and regional "seaweed" (marine grassroots)
   groups to mobilize voters in your congressional district and
   statewide in support of ocean-friendly issues and candidates. You can find these groups listed in the "Ocean and
   Coastal Conservation Guide" published by Blue Frontier and
   on its Web site (see Resources).

5. Attend an ocean conservation meeting or other gathering
   aimed at building an effective ocean constituency.

6. Contribute to the Ocean Champions political action com- mittee to help elect legislators who support ocean conservation.

7. Take a trip to Washington, DC as part of a blue delegation to lobby on behalf of ocean and coastal conservation. Before you go, check out "Ten Steps to a Successful Congressional Lobby Visit" at www.bluefront.org.

50. Be a Seaweed Rebel

A marine grassroots movement of concerned citizens—
a "seaweed" upsurge—can help you fight for healthy,
bountiful seas.

I remember reporting on a march at the 1992 Earth Summit in Rio de Janeiro, Brazil, where more than 190 heads of state had gathered. Thousands of local citizens and environmental activists from around the world streamed through this beautiful seaside city behind a banner reading "When the people lead, the leaders will follow."

We can all become leaders by changing our day-to-day behaviors in ways that demonstrate how to live well and sensibly on our blue-ocean planet. I hope this book will help you to do this. Beyond our individual choices, though, we need to become educators, adventure partners, and spiritual advisers to each other. Through organizations and citizen actions we can build a broad and effective voice for our living seas. By working to put the blue back in our red, white, and blue, we commit ourselves to a lifetime journey of rediscovery and a return to the sea—our greatest frontier and hope for restoration in the wake of tragedy and challenge. Nothing feels quite as rejuvenating as a fresh dip in the ocean. Take the plunge:

1. Go through this book, and make a checklist of how many things you're able to do. See if you can expand it.

2. Share this book with others you think might get involved in ocean work.

3. Choose one or several seaweed groups that you like, and commit some time to working with them.

4. Work on restoration efforts on the Gulf Coast and elsewhere that will lead to safer and more sustainable coastal communities.

5. Don't forget to go to the beach, jump into the ocean, and have some fun.

Acknowledgements

I'd like to thank the Center for the Study of Responsive Law, the Khaled bin Sultan Living Oceans Foundation, The Ocean Foundation, and other key supporters of the Blue Frontier Campaign that provided the opportunity to produce this book. Thanks to illustrator Jim Toomey for reaching out of his lagoon to add his fabulous pix, Philippe Cousteau for surfacing with his thoughtful foreword, the Blue Frontier volunteers, board, and staff who worked on and reviewed many of the book's sections, including Jean Logan, Jeff Oppenheimer, Diane Williams, Jon Christiansen, and Lea Bonfiglio. I also appreciated the stoked response from my agent, Keven Lyon, of the Dijkstra Literary Agency and Publisher Karen Bouris of Inner Ocean Publishing, who was thinking about 50 ways to save the ocean even before we sent the manuscript to her. And of course I'd like to thank the many sharks, stonefish, and monster waves who've allowed me to stay around long enough to finish this project. As naturalist author Ed Abbey used to say, "If there's not something bigger and meaner than you are out there, it's not really wilderness."

David Helvarg
President, Blue Frontier Campaign

Resources

section 1 Enjoy

....

1. Go to the Beach

> Clean Beaches Council
> www.cleanbeaches.org
> 1225 New York Avenue, NW, Suite 450
> Washington, DC 20005
> (202) 682-9507
> The council's Blue Wave certification helps the public iden-
> tify the nation's cleanest, safest, and most environmentally
> managed beaches.
>
> Natural Resources Defense Council
> www.nrdc.org
> 40 West 20th Street
> New York, NY 10011
> (212) 727-2700
> NRDC's annual report on water quality at beaches documents
> states and municipalities that have taken steps to reduce
> beach pollution or that have failed to protect swimmer safety
> and public health.

2. Get Married on a Wild Beach

> BeachBrideGuide.com
> www.beachbrideguide.com
> This Web site bills itself as the "largest Beach Wedding
> Resource on the Web" and offers suggestions, forums, and
> tips, along with a directory of local beach wedding listings
> and resources for different states.

Dr.Beach.org
www.drbeach.org
Laboratory for Coastal Research
Florida International University
University Park Campus
11200 SW 8th St., MARC 360
Miami, FL 33199
(305) 348-1339
Recognized throughout much of the world as "Dr. Beach," Dr. Stephen P. Leatherman has gained a reputation for his annual list of Top Ten Beaches. Every year he also lists the Best Wild Beaches in the United States.

3. Dive Responsibly

Reef Relief
www.reefrelief.org
PO Box 430
Key West, FL 33041
(305) 294-3100
Reef Relief is active in protecting water quality and developing community-based campaigns, including in-school programs, to protect coral reefs.

Project AWARE Foundation
www.projectaware.org
30151 Tomas Street, Suite 200
Rancho Santa Margarita, CA 92688
(949) 858-7657
Project AWARE is the dive industry's leading nonprofit environmental organization. Its Web site includes a number of environmental tips for divers.

4. Be a Blue Boater

Boat US (Boat Owners' Association of the United States).
www.boatus.com
880 South Pickett Street
Alexandria, VA 22304
(703) 823-9550
With 575,000 members, Boat US offers a range of services, including marine insurance, towing, product discounts, and a nonprofit foundation that promotes safe and environmentally sensitive recreational boating.

Blue Water Network
www.bluewaternetwork.org
311 California Street, Suite 510
San Francisco, CA 94104
(415) 544-0790
A leader in the campaign to find cleaner alternatives to two-stroke outboard engines, Blue Water Network also developed the first eco-labeling program for marine motors.

5. Keep Your Home Aquarium Ocean-Friendly

Reef Protection International
www.reefprotect.org
300 Broadway, Suite 28
San Francisco, CA 94103
(415) 788-3666, ext. 223
info@reefprotect.org
RPI educates consumers in the United States on how to maintain and assure environmentally friendly home aquariums. It is a good source of information before you make a purchase.

Marine Aquarium Council
www.aquariumcouncil.org
923 Nu'uanu Avenue
Honolulu, HI 96817
(808) 550-8217
MAC is creating standards and certifications (eco-labeling) for those engaged in the collection and care of ornamental marine life (to date, a very small part of the aquarium trade).

Washington, DC Area Marine Aquarist Society
www.wamas.org
PO Box 8831
Reston, VA 20195
WAMAS is an example of a local hobbyist group dedicated to husbandry of marine life in a captive environment in order to reduce the demand for wild-caught specimens. It also teaches the public about coral reefs and the ocean environment.

6. Go on a Whale-Watching Trip

American Cetacean Society
www.acsonline.org
PO Box 1391
San Pedro, CA 90733
(310) 548-6279
ACS works to protect whales, dolphins, porpoises, and their habitats through public education, research grants, and conservation actions. It also provides whale-watching opportunities and information.

Pacific Whale Foundation
www.pacificwhale.org
300 Maalaea Road, Suite 211
Wailuku, HI 96793
(808) 249-8811

The foundation combines research studies with nonprofit activism. Since 1980 nearly 2 million people have joined its eco-adventure cruises.

Greenpeace USA
www.greenpeace.org/usa
702 H Street NW
Washington, DC 20001
(202) 462-1177
Established in 1971 Greenpeace came to prominence blocking the harpoons of Russian Whalers. Today Greenpeace USA, among its many environmental efforts, is campaigning to end Japanese whaling in the southern Ocean.

7. Visit a Tide Pool

Between Pacific Tides,
Published by Stanford University Press
Stanford University Press
www.sup.org
1450 Page Mill Road
Palo Alto, CA 94304
(650) 723-9434
First published in 1939, and now in its fifth edition (1992), this classic reference on the rocky shores and tide pools of the Pacific Coast reflects the spirited personality of author Ed "Doc" Ricketts, the famed Monterey-based marine biologist.

Life at the Edge of the Sea, video
www.pbs.org/wnet/nature/edgeofsea
Made for the PBS series *Nature,* this documentary aired in 2000 but has left an impressive Web site in its wake. The site includes a Virtual Tide Pool tour that allows you to navigate through pools, click on various pool residents, and view them at both low and high tide.

8. Take Kids Surfing, or Have Them Take You

Surfrider Foundation
www.surfrider.org
PO Box 6010
San Clemente, CA 92674
(212) 727-2700
The foundation is a chapter-based group of thousands of surfers dedicated to the protection and enjoyment of the world's oceans, waves, and beaches.

Surfer magazine
www.surfermag.com
PO Box 1028
Dana Point, CA 92629
(949) 661-5150
Surfer began publication in 1960. Today it's considered the leading authority on all things wet, salty, and rideable. Not only did it help spawn a lifestyle and industry, but it was also the first surfing publication to raise warnings about environmental threats to the sport, and continues to do so.

Riding Giants, video
This 2004 wide-screen color documentary details the origin and history of surf culture, from its Polynesian roots to today's big money, big wave riding scene. Released in DVD in January 2005 by Columbia Tristar Home, and rated PG-13, it's available for sale or rental at most video rental stores.

Surfers Environmental Alliance
www.seasurfer.org
This alliance is an all-volunteer, grassroots group dedicated to the cultural and environmental integrity of surfing. It's based in Northern California and New Jersey.

9. Fish for Fun, Food, and the Future

National Coalition for Marine Conservation
www.savethefish.org
4 Royal Street, SE
Leesburg. VA 20175
(703) 777-0037
NCMC is a conservation group founded by recreational fishermen and women who wanted to make sure there would always be plenty of fish in the sea.

Coastal Conservation Association
www.joincca.org
6919 Portwest, Suite 100
Houston, TX 77024
(713) 626-4234
CCA advises and educates the public on conserving marine resources. It counts tens of thousands of recreational saltwater anglers among its membership. While it has been an active advocate for oceans, its recent criticism of no-take marine wilderness parks has put it at odds with other ocean conservationists.

10. Walk on Whatever Beach You Want

Coastal States Organization
www.coastalstates.org
Hall of the States, Suite 322
444 North Capitol Street, NW
Washington, DC 20001
(202) 508-3860
Formed in 1970, CSO represents the interest of the governors of the 35 coastal states, commonwealths, and territories of the United States. One of its efforts is to put the public trust doctrine to work.

Citizens Right to Access Beaches (CRAB)
www.crabnj.com
PO Box 1064
Point Pleasant Beach, NJ 08742
(732) 714-2722
Formed in 1996 over plans to restrict access to a public beach in Point Pleasant Beach, New Jersey, CRAB, like similar citizen groups along the coast, is dedicated to educating the public on its rights under the public trust doctrine.

11. Talk about the Ocean in Your Place of Worship

National Religious Partnership for the Environment
www.nrpe.org
49 South Pleasant St.
Suite 301
Amherst, MA 01002
The partnership is a formal alliance of major faith groups and denominations across the spectrum of Jewish and Christian communities in the United States. It is integrating care for God's creation throughout religious life: theology, worship, social teaching, education, congregational life, and public policy.

National Council of Churches USA Eco-justice Program
www.nccecojustice.org
Ecojustice Programs
National Council of Churches
110 Maryland Ave. NE
Washington DC 20002
The National Council of Churches represents 45 million Christians in 100,000 congregations. Its Eco-Justice Program has included a 2005 Earth Day Sunday focus on "Sacred Oceans and Seas" and a 2006 focus on rebuilding Gulf Coast Communities in the wake of Hurricanes Katrina and Rita.

. . . .

1 2. Eat Organic and Vegetarian Foods

> Institute for Agriculture and Trade Policy
> www.iatp.org
> 2105 First Avenue South
> Minneapolis, MN 55404
> (612) 870-0453
> IATP helps consumers make safe food choices and provides
> farmers with markets for healthy food.

> Organic Consumers Association
> www.organicconsumers.org
> 6101 Cliff Estate Road
> Litlle Marais, MN 55614
> (218) 226-4164
> OCA provides useful information on organic foods, family
> farms, and the environment.

1 3. Eat Seafood That's Healthy and Sustainable

> Seafood Choices Alliance
> www.seafoodchoices.com
> 1731 Connecticut Avenue, NW, 4th Floor
> Washington, DC 20009
> (202) 483-9570
> The alliance provides the information you need for making
> sound choices about seafood.

> Seafood Watch, Monterey Bay Aquarium
> www.mbayaq.org/cr/seafoodwatch.asp
> 886 Cannery Row
> Monterey, CA 93940
> (866) 732-6673

The mission of this program is to support sustainable fishing and aquaculture operations. It provides "Seafood Watch" pocket guides.

Marine Stewardship Council
www.msc.org
2110 North Pacific Street, Suite 102
Seattle, WA 98103
(206) 691-0188
The MSC rewards seafood caught by environmentally responsible methods with a distinctive blue product label.

Chefs Collaborative
www.chefscollaborative.org
262 Beacon Street
Boston, MA 02116
(617) 236-5200
The collaborative works with chefs to promote local, seasonal, and sustainable cuisine. Its member restaurants (listed on its Web site) serve sustainable seafood.

Blue Ocean Institute
www.blueoceaninstitute.org
250 Lawrence Hill Road
Cold Spring Harbor, NY 11724
(631) 367-0063
The Blue Ocean Institute's "Sea to Table" program includes publication of the *Seafood Lover's Almanac* and a seafood guide that explains the conservation status of different edible fish.

Environmental Defense
www.environmentaldefense.org
257 Park Ave. South
New York, NY 10010
(212)505-2100

Environmental Defense seeks innovative, pratical ways to solve urgent environmental problems through its "oceans alive" programs and others.

14. Grow a Natural Yard and Garden (and Play on a Natural Green)

Organic Gardening Magazine
www.organicgardening.com
400 South 10th St.
Emmaus, PA 18098
(610) 967-8363
This bimonthly publication gives useful information on how to grow anything you choose without chemicals.

Friends of Casco Bay
www.cascobay.org
43 Slocum Drive
South Portland, ME 04106
(207) 799-8574
Among the projects of this leading environmental organization in Casco Bay, Maine, is training master gardeners to become master bayscapers.

United States Golf Association
www.usga.org
The USGA acts as the national governing body for golf in the U.S. and Mexico and seeks to promote "environmentally-sensitive" golf courses.

15. Conserve Water

H2OUse.org
www.H2OUse.org
This site, created by the California Urban Water Conser-vation Council, is a virtual encyclopedia of water-saving tips and provides detailed, room-by-room breakdowns on how to reduce your water use, saving money and energy in the process.

WaterWiser
www.awwa.org/waterwiser
WaterWiser labels itself the "Water Efficiency Clearing-house." It's a fascinating Web site with links to all kinds of water education and conservation information, from fruit tree irrigation to how to reduce evaporation from your swimming pool.

16. Conserve Energy to Help the Seas and Yourself

Energy Star Program, Environmental Protection Agency,
Climate Protection Partnerships Division
www.energystar.gov
1200 Pennsylvania Avenue, NW
Washington DC 20460
(888) 782-7937
This EPA program helps businesses and individuals protect the environment through superior energy efficiency. In 2004, Energy Star helped save enough energy to power 20 million homes.

Home Energy Magazine
www.homeenergy.org
2124 Kittredge Street, #95
Berkeley, CA 94704
(510) 524-5405
This bimonthly magazine provides practical information on residential energy efficiency, performance, comfort, and affordability. Its do-it-yourself section and clear writing style appeal to the average home tinkerer.

17. Be a Marine Sanctuary Volunteer

National Marine Sanctuary Program, National Oceanic and
Atmospheric Administration.
www.sanctuaries.nos.noaa.gov

1305 East-West Highway, 11 th Floor
Silver Spring, MD. 20910
(301) 713-3125
The sanctuary program's mission is to conserve, protect, and enhance the biological diversity, ecological integrity, and cultural legacy of the system of marine reserves open to the public.

National Marine Sanctuary Foundation
www.nmsfocean.org
8601 Georgia Avenue, Suite 501
Silver Spring, MD 20910
(301) 608-3044
The foundation is working to establish a National Marine Sanctuary Volunteer Program to serve the different sanctuaries' needs and bring recognition to the thousands of people already working as volunteers.

Farallones Marine Sanctuary Association
www.farallones.org
The Presidio, PO Box 29386
San Francisco, CA 94129
(415) 561-6625
The association and its Beach Watch Program were the first locally developed volunteer efforts within the marine sanctuary system. Its citizen beach walkers carry out long-term monitoring of the sanctuary coastline and educate community members about the coast.

18. Prevent Sea Turtles from Going the Way of Dinosaurs

Sea Turtle Restoration Project
www.Seaturtles.org
PO Box 400
Forest Knolls, CA 94933
(415) 488-0370

STRP fights to protect endangered sea turtle populations through grassroots action and community-based organizing that you can be a part of.

Caribbean Conservation Corporation and Sea Turtle Survival League
www.cccturtle.org
4424 NW 13th Street, Suite A-1
Gainesville, FL 32609
(800) 678-7853
Founded by Dr. Archie Carr in 1959, this group offers people an opportunity to volunteer for turtle protection patrols, participate in research projects, or "adopt a turtle" that's being tracked by satellite.

The International Ecotourism Society
www.ecotourism.org
733 15th Street, NW, Suite 1000
Washington, DC 20005
(202) 347-9203
TIES is the largest and oldest ecotourism organization in the world. It provides assistance designed to make tourism a tool for conservation of the environment, alleviation of poverty, and protection of culture, as well as for enjoyment.

19. Use Less Plastic

Algalita Marine Research Foundation
www.algalita.org
148 Marina Drive
Long Beach, CA 90803
(562) 598-4889
AMRF's research on pelagic plastics first identified the presence of six pounds of plastic for every pound of zooplankton in the North Pacific.

Industrial Agricultural Products Center, University of Nebraska
http://agproducts.unl.edu
208 L.W. Chase Hall
Lincoln, NE 68583
(402) 472-1634
This research center is one of a growing network of labs, companies, and retail outlets providing plastic products made from corn and other agricultural materials. Unlike petroleum-based plastics, these "green plastics" break down naturally in terrestrial and marine environments.

20. Opt Out of the Throwaway Culture

Center for a New American Dream
www.newdream.org
6930 Carroll Avenue, Suite 900
Takoma Park, MD 20912
(301) 891-3683
The center helps Americans consume responsibly to protect the environment, enhance quality of life, and promote social justice. It works with individuals, communities, and businesses to counter the commercialization of our culture.

Simple Living Network
www.simpleliving.net
This Web site offers many useful tools for people who want to follow the spirit of Thoreau by reducing the clutter in their lives, their environmental footprint, and their dependence on mainstream corporate culture to define what makes them happy.

21. Raise Funds for Ocean Conservation

The Foundation Center
www.fdncenter.org
79 Fifth Avenue at 16th Street
New York, NY 10003
(212) 620-4230

The center is the nation's leading authority on philanthropy. Its information services and libraries are a vital resource for grant-seekers, grant-givers, researchers, journalists, and interested citizens.

Charity Navigator
www.charitynavigator.org
1200 MacArthur Boulevard, Second Floor
Mahwah, NJ 07430
(201) 818-1288
Charity Navigator helps charitable givers make decisions by providing information on more than 4,000 charities and evaluating the financial health of each of them. Its Web site is easy to understand and freely available to the public. Presently it lists fewer than 100 of more than 1,000 nonprofits involved in ocean conservation, although the number is likely to increase.

section 3 Clean

. . . .

22. Maintain an Ocean-Friendly Driveway or Green Roof

www.Greenbuilder.com/sourcebook
This online resource fosters environmentally responsible practices in home building, including how to find and install "pervious" paving materials, which allow water to seep through.

Green Building Council
www.usgbc.org
1015 18th Street, NW, Suite 508
Washington, DC 20036
(202) 828-7422
The council works to promote buildings that are environmentally healthy places to live and work.

Greenroofs.com
www.Greenroofs.com
3449 Lakewind Way
Alpharetta, GA 30005
(678) 580-1965
This clearinghouse for the green roof movement publishes an online "Greenroof Directory of Manufacturers, Suppliers, Professional Services, Organizations, Students, and Green Resources."

23. Keep Your Household Refuse Nontoxic

Washington Toxics Coalition
www.watoxics.org
4649 Sunnyside Avenue North, Suite 510
Seattle, WA 98103
(206) 632-1545
WTC is one of many local and state citizen groups working to protect public health. Its Web site has extensive information on toxics in the home and natural alternatives to them.

Green Building Supply
www.greenbuildingsupply.com
508 North 2nd Street
Fairfield, IA
(800) 405-0222
Green Building Supply is one of a growing number of shops and outlets for natural and ecological home building products, including environmentally friendly cleaners, nontoxic paints and finishes, and energy- and water-conserving appliances such as dishwashers, toilets, washing machines, and dryers.

Environmental Products for Important Causes
www.products4causes.com
PO Box 9254
San Diego, CA 92169
(858) 220-8288
EPIC sells natural, biodegradable, and non-petroleum-based fragrances, household cleaners, and industrial cleaning products, including soaps, degreasers, and scrubs. It donates all after-tax profits to environmental causes.

24. Drive a Fuel-Efficient Car, Join a Car Pool, or Use Public Transit

GreenerCars.com
www.greenercars.com
American Council for an Energy-Efficient Economy
1001 Connecticut Avenue, NW, Suite 801
Washington, DC 20036
(202) 429-8873
At this online resource, you'll find ACEEE's "Green Book," an environmental buyers' guide for different year and model cars and trucks, along with news, articles, and consumer advice.

Ecology Center of Michigan
www.ecocenter.org
117 North Division Street
Ann Arbor, MI 48104
(734) 761-3186
The center's Auto Project addresses toxic and health issues related to production of automobiles and promotes cleaner vehicle technologies.

Rocky Mountain Institute
www.rmi.org
1739 Snowmass Creek Road
Snowmass, CO 91654
(970) 927-3851

RMI is an innovative leader in the development of alternative-transportation technology and fuel-related issues.

eRideShare.com
www.eRideShare.com
PO Box 402
Edwardsville, IL 62025
(618) 530-4842
This Web site is a free nationwide source for finding a match for your commute. It lists nearly 15,000 carpools.

25. Don't Use Your Storm Drain as If It Were a Toilet

U.S. Environmental Protection Agency, Office of Wetlands, Oceans, and Watersheds
www.epa.gov/owow/
1200 Pennsylvania Avenue, NW
Washington, DC 20460
(202) 566-1300
EPA's Office of Wetlands, Oceans and Watersheds works on issues of polluted runoff including runoff from storm drains. Its Web site and regional offices offer resources that can help citizens reduce this major source of marine pollution.

California State Water Resources Control Board, Office of Public Affairs
www.swrcb.ca.gov/erasethewaste
1001 I Street
Sacramento, CA 95814
(916) 341-5254
The water board's storm-water public education campaign in Los Angeles, "Erase the Waste," is an example of how agencies can educate us to protect our beaches and coastal waters from storm-drain runoff.

Waterkeeper Alliance
www.waterkeeper.org
50 S. Buckhout St., Suite 302
Irvington, NY 10533
(914) 674-0622
Waterkeeper Alliance champions clean water through local waterkeeper programs nationally and worldwide.

26. Upgrade Your House above Hurricane Code

Miami-Dade County Product Control Division
www.miamidade.gov/buildingcode
Building Code Compliance Office
140 W. Flagler St., Ste 1603
Miami, FL 33130-1563
(305) 375-2901
The Product Control Division tests and certifies hurricane damage prevention equipment, from storm shutters and doors to roof systems, to make sure they meet a tough hurricane code. You can use its product-search feature to select a product likely to survive even the worst hurricane.

Institute for Business and Home Safety
www.ibhs.org
4775 East Fowler Avenue
Tampa, FL 33617
(813) 286-3400
IBHS provides advice about protecting businesses, homes, and communities from disasters, including hurricanes and coastal flooding.

27. Join in a Coastal Cleanup

The Ocean Conservancy
www.oceanconservancy.org
1725 DeSales Street, NW, Suite 600

Washington DC 20036
(202) 429-5609
Among its many projects, TOC sponsors the International
Coastal Cleanup and does work on a National Marine Debris
Monitoring Program that also seeks volunteers.

California Coastal Commission
www.coastal.ca.gov
45 Fremont Street, Suite 2000
San Francisco, CA 94105
(415) 904-5200
The CCC's annual Coastal Cleanup Day draws more than
40,000 volunteers to more than 700 cleanup sites. Its Adopt-
a-Beach program commits groups to cleaning beaches at least
three times a year.

28. Protect Our Waters from Invasive Organisms (Exotic Critters)

Marine Invasion Research Laboratory
www.serc.si.edu/labs/marine_invasions
PO Box 28
Edgewood, MD 21037
(443) 482-2414
Working as part of the Smithsonian Environmental Research
Center, this lab is a center for research on biological invasions in coastal and marine ecosystems and a source of much
valuable information.

A Plague of Rats and Rubber Vines,
published by Island Press
Island Press
www.islandpress.org
1718 Connecticut Avenue, NW, Suite 300
Washington, DC 20009
(202) 232-7933

This 2002 book provides an overview of the problem of harmful invasive or alien species—the world's "rats and rubber vines"—and offers possible solutions.

29. Sail on an Ocean-Friendly Cruise Ship

Oceana
www.oceana.org
2501 M Street, NW, Suite 300
Washington, D.C. 20037
(202) 833-3900
Among the international efforts of this marine environmental group is a Stop Cruise Ship Pollution campaign that seeks public participation to help clean up the industry.

National Response Center
www.nrc.uscg.mil
c/o United States Coast Guard (G-OPF), Room 2611
2100 2nd Street, SW
Washington, DC 20593
(800) 424-8802
The National Response Center is the single federal point of contact for reporting oil and chemical spills (and illegal ocean dumping) from cruise ships and other vessels. The NRC operates 24 hours a day, 7 days a week, 365 days a year.

section 4 Protect

· ·

30. Support Your Local Wetlands

Restore America's Estuaries
www.estuaries.org
3801 North Fairfax Drive, Suite 53
Arlington, VA 22203
(703) 524-0248

RAE produces a citizens' guide to estuarine and wetlands habitat restoration.

National Oceanic and Atmospheric Administration (NOAA) Restoration Center
www.nmfs.noaa.gov/habitat/restoration
1315 East-West Highway
Silver Spring, MD 20910
(301) 713-0174
The center's Community-Based Restoration Program has helped more than 1,500 local organizations restore marine and coastal habitats through projects providing both funds and expertise.

Friends of the Everglades
www.everglades.org
7800 Red Road, Suite 215K
Miami, FL 33143
(305) 669-0858
This group works to protect, restore, and preserve the Everglades ecosystem. By joining you can help renew the lifeblood of the "river of grass."

Ducks Unlimited
www.ducks.org
One Waterfowl Way
Memphis, TN 38120
(901) 758-3825
Ducks Unlimited conserves, restores, and manages wetlands and associated habitats for North America's waterfowl. The group's membership includes many duck hunters.

31. Restore a Stream, River, or Watershed

> **American Rivers**
> www.americanrivers.org
> 1025 Vermont Avenue, NW, Suite 720
> Washington, DC 20005
> (202) 347-7550
> This group has collaborated with many partners to develop a Citizens' Agenda for Rivers.

> **Center for Watershed Protection**
> www.cwp.org
> 8390 Main Street, 2nd Floor
> Ellicott City, MD 21043
> (410) 461-8323
> The center provides technical tools for protecting streams, lakes, and rivers. It has developed a strategy that includes planning, restoration, storm-water management, research, and training.

32. Live a Reasonable Distance from the Beach

> **Federal Emergency Management Agency**
> www.fema.gov
> 500 C Street, SW
> Washington, DC 20472
> (202) 566-1600
> Along with its other work, FEMA provides maps defining levels of flood risk for different areas.

> *Coastal Living* **Magazine**
> www.coastalliving.com
> 2100 Lakeshore Drive
> Birmingham, AL 35209
> (205) 445-6007
> Geared to "people who love the coast," this magazine runs regular features on ways to build in harmony with nature and assure a secure and lasting place to live by the sea.

33. Count the Fish; Then Do Some Light Housekeeping for Them

Reef Environmental Education Foundation
www.reef.org
PO Box 246
Key Largo, FL 33037
(305) 852-0030
REEF members regularly conduct fish biodiversity and abundance surveys. The foundation also maintains a database generated by the Great Annual Fish Count, for use by citizens and scientists.

Coral Reef Alliance (CORAL)
www.coral.org
417 Montgomery Street, Suite 205
San Francisco, CA 94104
(415) 834-0900
CORAL promotes coral reef conservation. Its Web site includes how-to guides and resources for underwater cleanups.

Marine Fish Conservation Network
www.conservefish.org
600 Pennsylvania Ave. SE, Suite 210
Washington, DC 20003
(202) 543-5509
This network is a coalition of over 170 groups of environmental organizations, fishing groups, aquariums, and others dedicated to conserving and sustaining marine fish.

34. Protect the Dunes So They'll Protect Us

American Littoral Society
www.littoralsociety.org
Sandy Hook
Highlands, NJ 07732
(732) 291-0055

ALS gets its name from the Latin *litus,* meaning beach or coastal. It's concerned about issues that affect the area between the low and high tide lines, including various types of dune systems.

Dunes Center
www.dunescenter.org
1055 Guadalupe Street
Guadalupe, CA 93434
(805) 343-2455
The center carries out educational, research, and conservation activities in support of the Guadalupe-Nipomo Dunes Complex, 18 miles of the largest, most diverse coastal dune/lagoon ecosystem on earth.

35. Power Down around Whales, Manatees, and Other Marine Wildlife

Save the Manatee Club
www.savethemanatee.org
500 North Maitland Avenue, Suite 210
Maitland, FL 32751
(800) 432-5646
SMC was started to enable the public to participate in efforts to save endangered manatees. Its Adopt-a-Manatee program donations and other resources go toward public education, research, rescue, and rehabilitation activities.

Marine Mammal Commission
www.mmc.gov
4340 East-West Highway, Suite 905
Bethesda, MD 20814
(301) 504-0087
This independent agency of the federal government can provide you with information and contacts about how to interact safely with manatees, dolphins, whales, and other marine mammals.

36. Join a Marine Mammal Rescue Center

Office of Protected Resources, National Marine Fisheries Service
www.nmfs.noaa.gov/pr/health
1315 East-West Highway, 13th Floor
Silver Spring, MD 20910
(301) 713-2332
The office's Stranding Response Program authorizes the activities of volunteer marine mammal stranding networks that rescue and rehabilitate marine wildlife.

Marine Mammal Center
www.marinemammalcenter.org
Marin Headlands
1065 Fort Cronkhite
Sausalito, CA 94965
(415) 289-7325
Formed by three volunteers in 1975, this center has rescued and treated more than 9,000 animals. Each year, along with recruiting volunteers, it educates more than 60,000 school-children and members of the public.

Marine Mammal Conservancy
www.marinemammalconservancy.org
P.O. Box 1625
Key Largo, FL 33037
(305) 451-4774
The conservancy works to provide professional and effective response and care for stranded marine mammals.

37. Work to Create Wilderness Parks under the Sea

Marine Protected Areas of the United States
www.mpa.gov
1305 East-West Highway
Silver Spring, MD 20910
(301) 713-3100 ext. 195

In 2000, a presidential executive order mandated creation of a system of marine protected areas in federal waters. NMPAC was established to implement the order. It could use more public input.

Marine Reserves: A Guide to Science, Design and Use,
published by Island Press
Island Press
www.islandpress.org
1718 Connecticut Avenue, NW, Suite 300
Washington, DC 20009
(202) 232-7933

While not a casual read, this 2004 book provides a complete guide to no-take marine reserves. Global in perspective, it includes case studies from California, Belize, and the Bahamas.

38. Don't Feed the Sharks (or Let Them Feed on You)

Shark Research Institute
www.sharks.org
PO Box 40
Princeton, NJ 08540
(609) 921-3522

SRI conducts scientific research on sharks and promotes their conservation. It has field offices around the world and undertakes research expeditions that certified divers can participate in.

International Shark Attack File
www.flmnh.ufl.edu/fish/sharks/isaf/isaf.htm
Florida Museum of Natural History
University of Florida
Gainesville, FL 32611
(352) 392-1721

While many shark species are threatened with extinction at human hands, people are still fascinated with sharks, largely because of their occasional attacks on us. The International Shark Attack File is a compilation of all known shark attacks going back to the mid-1500s. Full access is granted to qualified researchers. The press and public can also access nonsensitive information.

39. Don't Exploit Sea Creatures for Vanity's Sake

Environmental Investigation Agency
www.eia-international.org
PO Box 53343
Washington, DC 20009
(202) 483-6621

EIA investigates, exposes, and campaigns against the illegal trade in wildlife, including marine wildlife. Working undercover, EIA has directly brought about changes in international law.

Project Seahorse
www.projectseahorse.org
Fisheries Centre
University of British Columbia
2202 Main Mall
Vancouver BC, V6T 1Z4 Canada
(604) 827-5139

This international organization is committed to the conservation and sustainable use of coastal marine ecosystems where sea horses are found. Among its partner groups is the Shedd Aquarium in Chicago.

40. Keep Oil off Our Shore

National OCS Coalition
P.O. Box 583
Bodega Bay, CA 94923
(707) 875-2345
waterway@monitor.net
This coalition is led by longtime ocean advocate Richard
Charter, who has spent more than 30 years linking activists,
the public, and elected officials working to prevent reckless
offshore oil and gas development on the Outer Continental
Shelf (OCS).

Natural Energy Laboratory of Hawaii Authority
www.nelha.org
73-4460 Queen Kaahumanu Highway, #101
Kailua-Kona, HI 96740
(808) 329-7341
NELHA is a state agency that operates a unique 870-acre
ocean science and technology park on the Big Island of
Hawaii. It pumps deep, cold, nutrient-rich ocean waters to
land for use in aquaculture and medical research. It also has
the potential to generate clean energy by using temperature
differences between deep and surface waters. Daily tours of
NELHA are open to the public.

The Hydrogen Economy,
published by Jeremy P. Tarcher/Putnam
Penguin Putnam, Inc.
www.penguinputnam.com
375 Hudson Street
New York, NY 10014
This thought-provoking book examines the rise and fall of the
oil economy and posits an emerging system of sustainable
energy production based on hydrogen fuel-cell technology. It's
an easy read on a tough and challenging topic.

. . . .

41. Visit an Aquarium

The American Zoo and Aquarium Association
www.aza.org
8403 Colesville Road, Suite 710
Silver Spring, MD 20910
(301) 562-0777
AZA is dedicated to excellence in animal care and welfare, conservation, education, research, and public respect for animals and nature.

The Ocean Project
www.seastheday.org
PO Box 2506
Providence, RI 02906
(401) 709-4071
Through collaboration among aquariums, zoos, science museums, and natural history museums, the Ocean Project seeks to involve people actively in conservation in their communities and better connect them to the oceans.

42. Support Marine Education in Our Schools

National Marine Educators Association
www.vims.edu/nmea
PO Box 1470
Ocean Springs, MS 39566
NMEA provides a focus for marine and aquatic studies. It is affiliated with the National Science Teachers Association and the American Association for the Advancement of Science.

The Jason Project
www.jason.org
44983 Knoll Square
Ashburn, VA 20147
(703) 726-8279
The foundation's mission is to inspire in students a lifelong passion for science, math, and technology through hands-on, real-world scientific discovery involving the seas.

EarthEcho International
www.earthecho.org
1050 Connecticut Avenue, NW, Suite 1000
Washington, DC 20036
(202) 772-4272
Among other activities, EarthEcho offers a series of educational curriculums (for classrooms and home schooling) combining traditional printed teaching tools with interactive online distance learning and high-quality documentaries about our oceans.

Khaled bin Sultan Living Oceans Foundation
www.livingoceansfoundation.org
8181 Professional Place, Suite 215
Landover, MD 20785
(301) 577-1288
The Living Oceans Foundation works to conserve and restore living oceans through research, education, and commitment to "science without borders."

43. Speak for the Seas at Local Public Hearings

American Planning Association
www.planning.org
122 South Michigan Avenue, Suite 1600
Chicago, IL 60603
(312) 431-9100

APA works to advance the art and science of environmentally sustainable planning for cities, towns, and other areas.

Smart Growth Network
www.smartgrowth.org
c/o International City/County Management Association
777 North Capitol Street, NE, Suite 500
Washington, DC 20002
(202) 962-3623
The network's activities raise public awareness, promote smart-growth best practices, provide information, and develop sensible growth strategies. Its partners include both citizen activists and government organizations.

44. Learn Your Local Maritime History

Mystic Seaport
www.mysticseaport.org
PO Box 60000
75 Greenmanville Avenue
Mystic, CT 06355
(888) 973-2767
Connecticut's Mystic Seaport labels itself "The Museum of America and the Sea." It's notable both for its collection of sailing ships and boats and for its re-creation of an entire 19th-century seaport, including a shipyard. It also has an extensive research collection and offers a range of activities, from day visits to sailing classes to graduate courses on American maritime history.

Hawai'i Maritime Center
http://holoholo.org/maritime
Pier 7, Honolulu Harbor
Honolulu, HI 96813
(808) 523- 6151

This center is an outstanding maritime museum, from its boathouse exhibits of Hawaii's past to its whaling artifacts, surfboards, and sea vessels. The latter include the *Hokulea,* a double-hulled sailing canoe that re-created the Polynesian Voyage of Discovery, and the *Falls of Clyde* a four-masted schooner that used to run tea from China.

Shifting Baselines
www.shiftingbaselines.org
5254 Melrose Avenue, Suite D-112
Hollywood, CA 90038
(323) 960-4517

Shifting Baselines is a media project to call public attention to the swift pace of ocean life decline. Among its tools are humorous public service announcements, short films, and a lively Web site.

45. Talk to Your Cousin in Kansas about the Weather

Mississippi River Basin Alliance
www.mrba.org
2104 Stevens Avenue South
Minneapolis, MN 55404
(612) 879-7540

The alliance is a coalition of more than 150 grassroots organizations, from the headwaters of northern Minnesota to the battered Gulf of Mexico, working to save the Mississippi River and the ocean it feeds into.

Farm Aid
www.farmaid.org
11 Ward Street, Suite 200
Somerville, MA 02143
(617) 354-2922

Farm Aid brings together family farmers and citizens to restore family farm agriculture, believing that this ensures safe, healthful food, protects natural resources, and strengthens local economies. Among its programs is an annual concert.

46. Learn How to Navigate and Read the Tides

National Ocean Service and National Geospatial Agency
http://oceanservice.noaa.gov
http://nga.mil
These two federal agencies provide the most accurate and information-rich nautical charts. NOS publishes about 1,000 charts for United States waters; NGA issues charts of the high seas and other nations' waters. You can purchase the charts in most marine supply stores.

Sea Scouts
www.seascout.org
Sea Scouting is a coeducational program of Boy Scouts of America offered to young adults between 14 and 21. It promotes citizenship and improves members' boating skills and knowledge of the sea. To find a local Sea Scout unit (called a "ship") go to the Sea Scout Web site.

47. Immerse Yourself in Blue Media

Public Broadcast System (PBS) and National Geographic
www.shoppbs.org
www.shop.nationalgeographic.com
These are two good sources for finding ocean books and videos to buy. A search through www.Amazon.com or your local video store, independent bookstore, or public library may turn up some hidden blue treasures as well.

Coney Island Mermaid Parade
www.coneyisland.com/mermaid.shtml
1208 Surf Avenue
Brooklyn, NY 11224-2816
(718) 372-5159

San Clemente Ocean Festival
www.oceanfestival.org
PO Box 1373
San Clemente, CA 92674
(949) 440-6141

48. Go on a Live or Virtual Ocean Expedition

National Oceanic and Atmospheric Administration's Ocean
Explorer
http://oceanexplorer.noaa.gov
1315 East-West Highway, 10th floor
Silver Spring, MD 20910
(301) 713-9444

This program is designed to search and investigate the deepest reaches of our oceans and to share its findings with the world. For some amazing images of "alien" life on our planet, or to learn ways you can get involved, go to its Web site.

NOAA's Aquarius
www.uncw.edu/aquarius
National Undersea Research Center
University of North Carolina, Wilmington
515 Caribbean Drive
Key Largo, FL 33035
(305) 451-0233

Aquarius, billed as "America's Innerspace Station," is an underwater ocean laboratory located in the Florida Keys National Marine Sanctuary. Scientists live in and conduct saturation diving from Aquarius during ten-day missions. The program's Web site often includes live links to the station.

Earthwatch Institute
www.earthwatch.org
3 Clock Tower Place, Suite 100
Box 75
Maynard, MA 01754
(800) 776-0188
Earthwatch engages members of the public in scientific field research to promote understanding and action for a sustainable environment. It has 130 expeditions working in 47 countries.

49. Vote for Those Who Protect the Coast

Vote the Coast
www.votethecoast.org
PO Box 1022
Malibu, CA 90265
(310) 456 5674
This California grassroots political action organization supports candidates for public office who are guided by principles of ecological sustainability, environmental justice, public education, participatory governance, commitment, and integrity.

Ocean Champions
www.oceanchampions.org
c/o David Wilmot, President
202 San Jose Avenue
Capitola, CA 95010
(831) 462-2539
Ocean Champions and its political action committee aim to develop a bipartisan base of supporters from which to cultivate (and help finance) political champions for ocean conservation in Congress and key states.

50. Be a Seaweed Rebel

Blue Frontier Campaign
www.bluefront.org
PO Box 19367
Washington, DC 20036
(202) 387-8030
The campaign works to strengthen the United States ocean constituency by building unity, providing tools, and heightening awareness of our public seas and solutions for restoring them. It seeks to establish broad coalitions of "seaweed" (marine grassroots) activists to enact comprehensive ocean-protection legislation, policies, and ethics from sea to shining sea.

Ocean and Coastal Conservation Guide 2005–2006,
published by Island Press
Island Press
www.islandpress.org
1718 Connecticut Avenue, NW, Suite 300
Washington, DC 20009
(202) 232-7933
Compiled biannually by the Blue Frontier Campaign, this comprehensive guide to the new "blue movement" details more than 2,000 organizations working to understand, protect, and restore our oceans and coastal areas. Along with state-by-state contact information and descriptions, the directory includes detailed sections identifying relevant government agencies, academic marine programs, and marine and coastal parks.

Also available from Inner Ocean Publishing

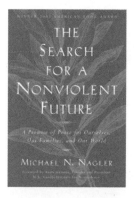

**THE SEARCH FOR A
NONVIOLENT FUTURE**
*A Promise of Peace for Ourselves,
Our Families, and Our World*
Michael N. Nagler

**MOVEON'S 50 WAYS TO
LOVE YOUR COUNTRY**
*How to Find Your Political Voice and
Become a Catalyst for Change*
MoveOn.org

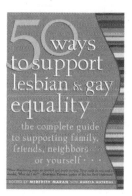

**50 WAYS TO SUPPORT
LESBIAN & GAY EQUALITY**
*The Complete Guide to Supporting
Family, Neighbors—or Yourself*
Meredith Maran
with Angela Watrous

**50 WAYS TO IMPROVE
WOMEN'S LIVES**
*The Essential Women's Guide for
Achieving Health, Equality, and Success*
National Council of
Women's Organizations